WIND POWER

20 Projects to Make with Paper

CLIVE DOBSON

WIND POWER

20 Projects to Make with Paper

CLIVE DOBSON

FIREFLY BOOKS

A FIREFLY BOOK

Published by Firefly Books Ltd. 2010

The publisher gratefully acknowledges the financial support for our publishing program by the Government of Canada through the Canada Book Fund as administered by the Department of Canadian Heritage.

First printing

Library and Archives Canada Cataloguing in Publication

Dobson, Clive, 1949-
Wind power : 20 projects to make with paper / Clive Dobson.
Includes bibliographical references and index.
ISBN-13: 978-1-55407-749-6 (pbk.)   ISBN-10: 1-55407-749-4 (pbk.)
ISBN-13: 978-1-55407-659-8 (bound)   ISBN-10: 1-55407-659-5 (bound)
1. Wind power--Juvenile literature. 2. Paper work--Juvenile literature. I. Title.
TJ820.D62 2010   j621.31'2136   C2010-903669-7

Publisher Cataloging-in-Publication Data (U.S.)

Dobson, Clive.
Wind power : 20 projects to make with paper / Clive Dobson.
[96] p. : ill. (some col.), col. photos. ; cm.
Includes bibliographic references and index.
Summary: Projects for youth that use, adapt and illustrate the power of the wind. Includes a basic scientific understanding of wind power and the ways in which it can be harnessed for vital tasks that require energy.
ISBN-13: 978-1-55407-749-6 (pbk.)   ISBN-10: 1-55407-749-4 (pbk.)
ISBN-13: 978-1-55407-659-8 (bound)   ISBN-10: 1-55407-659-5 (bound)
1. Wind power – Juvenile literature. 2. Science projects – Juvenile literature. I. Title.
621.45 dc22   TJ820.D6376 2010

Published in the United States by
Firefly Books (U.S.) Inc.
P.O. Box 1338, Ellicott Station,
Buffalo, New York 14205

Published in Canada by
Firefly Books Ltd.
66 Leek Crescent,
Richmond Hill, Ontario L4B 1H1

Cover design: McCorkindale Advertising & Design
Interior design, back cover and production: Chris McCorkindale and Sue Breen, McCorkindale Advertising & Design
Photography editing by Jolie Dobson Photography

Printed in China

› Contents

> INTRODUCTION

As the true method of knowledge is experiment the true faculty of knowing must be the faculty which experiences. — William Blake, 1788

Although this quote from the poet William Blake is taken out of its original context, it is relevant to the intentions of this book. Through experimentation with pinwheels and other small turbines you design and make for yourself out of simple materials and using basic geometry, you can learn more about the power of wind. You can experience the properties of moving air on various forms and discover through trial and error what makes them effective — or not — for toys, artwork, kinetic power and even for generating electricity. The forms your projects can take are almost as infinite and limitless as the wind itself.

The real hands-on experience you gain in trying out different materials, shapes and sizes will be the best teacher you could ever have. And the more you learn about wind power, the more you will believe that some day you might use it in your daily life.

There is a lot of public interest today in living a more sustainable lifestyle and seeking out renewable sources of energy. As electric utilities become less regulated by governments, there are opportunities to consider alternative sources of electricity. In the past few years solar-powered cells and wind-powered generators have gained acceptance worldwide as practical ways to solve our ever-increasing demand for energy.

New and old: Giant wind turbines generating electrical power and a ranch water-pumping windmill at Rio Vista, California.

The rush to build wind farms in the name of clean energy has made it easy for wind energy developers to convince the public that a wind farm in their area could be their salvation from global warming. However, more and more information is surfacing about the ill effects from the noise that wind farms are having on people who live close to large wind turbines. And there is the danger that these turbines will become the next generation of eyesores, much like the high-tension power transmission lines that already cut across cities and quiet rural areas. There is a need to use smaller, quieter wind generators instead of allowing the proliferation of giant industrial wind turbines.

Excellent innovative technology does exist to manufacture small, quieter wind generators for individual household use. Looking into the future, it is easy to see a day when new homes may come equipped with their own built-in wind-powered systems for generating electricity, perhaps beginning with a generator that could provide back-up power in an emergency and also recharge electric vehicles. Such systems could allow anyone to become more self sufficient and at the same time make a contribution to reducing carbon emissions.

Will future generations be able to see clear blue sky and breathe clean fresh air because of these smaller wind-powered generators? Perhaps they will. It is my hope that this book of simple projects will help further an interest in the development of small wind devices, especially among the young and the young at heart, who are the most natural and enthusiastic of experimenters.

〉WIND

The power of the Sun

The Sun is the powerhouse of our planet Earth. The heat of the Sun warms the surface of the Earth and is absorbed by land and bodies of water during the day. But land and water absorb heat and release heat differently. And warm air rises because it is lighter than cold air. As the warm air rises, cooler air moves in to take the place of the warmer air. So warm and cold air circulate all the time in currents of air — wind — in a process called convection.

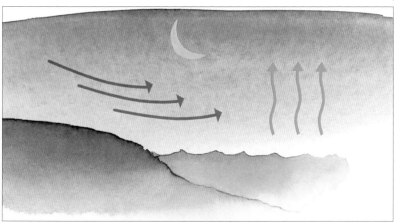

During the day, warm air rises over land heated by the Sun to produce an on-shore breeze. (The air is moving from a high-pressure zone to a low-pressure zone.) At night, the process is reversed. Since land cools down faster than the ocean, the wind often changes direction in the evening when you are near the coast.

The uneven heating of the Earth's surface produces high-pressure and low-pressure zones. When air moves from a high-pressure zone to a low-pressure zone, wind is the result.

The illustrations here show on a small scale how the Sun creates high- and low-pressure differences over land and water and how the wind changes direction.

Prevailing winds

Prevailing winds are winds that mostly blow from one direction throughout the year. During the age of sail, when most travel of any great distance was by sailing ship, prevailing winds made it possible to easily make a round trip across an ocean and back. Sailing ships relied upon a northern-latitude westerly wind to cross the Atlantic to Europe and a southerly trade wind to return.

In the northern hemisphere, weather systems generally move from the west in an eastward direction due to the prevailing westerlies. When a high-pressure, dry polar outflow of air collides with a low-pressure, humid air mass from the southwest, the warm humid air from the southwest is forced up over the dense dry cold air, forming clouds that release rain or snow.

Within these weather systems, local winds at ground level can come from any direction, even the east (against prevailing westerlies), but still the whole system moves eastward.

Active weather forms frequently along the edge of a polar outflow of air that has moved southward. This is called a polar front. A cold polar front can move from northern Canada as far south as Florida during the winter months and can cause great damage to orange crops. During spring and summer, the collision of a polar front with a warm humid air mass from the Gulf of Mexico can produce violent updrafts, torrential thunderstorms and tornadoes. This is a predictable factor that must be considered when engineering any permanent wind device.

Prevailing winds in any region are the most reliable winds and that makes them the best winds to be harnessed to drive windmills and wind turbines.

How do you know what direction the wind is coming from? One easy sailor's trick is to wet your finger and hold it up in the air. The side that feels colder is where the wind is coming from.

A more reliable way to read wind direction on land is by using a wind vane, often called a weather vane, since a change in wind direction can also indicate a change in weather. Because weather plays a critical role in daily activities and the development of crops, farms often have a weather vane in the form of a rotating rooster perched atop the barn roof. The rooster revolves around the four fixed main compass points — north, east, south and west — and the force of the wind keeps it pointed in one direction, at least until the wind shifts. In a conventional weather vane, the head of the rooster points in the direction the wind is coming from.

Seeing wind

Just as we can't see air, likewise we can't see wind. However, we can see water vapor in the air in its many forms (clouds, fog, rain, snow and steam) and we are aware of wind when these suspended elements move. Everyone has observed clouds racing across the sky on a windy day or the horizontal drift of falling snow during the winter months. We are aware of the wind when we see smoke drifting sideways, when the leaves rustle in the trees, when we feel it on our faces, and when it makes a whistling sound in the wires along our street. We see its force at work on a sailboat moving across the horizon far out at sea, or in the spinning blades of a wind turbine.

On rare occasions the unleashed force of the wind can cause great destruction, as when a hurricane slams into a coastal region flooding cities and towns with a tidal surge, blowing the roofs off buildings, uprooting trees and filling the screaming air with flying debris.

In this photograph of a weather vane and anemometer, the wind is coming from the southeast.

Measuring wind

In 1805 Sir Francis Beaufort devised a universal way to estimate nautical wind speed and the force of the wind. He created a numbered scale so that these conditions could be entered into a ship's log when it was at sea. This scale has been in use ever since and has become a standard worldwide.

At right is the Beaufort Scale, with descriptions added to show the effects of each category on land. When a storm is described as having wind force 8 or more, you had better run for cover!

Today, wind speed is measured using an instrument called an anemometer. There are also other scales used to classify wind force, especially when it comes to tropical cyclones. The Saffir-Simpson Hurricane Scale is one. To learn more about extreme weather and how it is measured, go to the website of the World Meteorological Organization, at www.wmo.int.

THE BEAUFORT WIND FORCE SCALE

Wind Force	Wind Speed (mph)	Wind Description
0	Less than 1	Calm
1	1–3	Light air
2	4–7	Light breeze
3	8–12	Gentle breeze
4	13–18	Moderate breeze
5	19–24	Fresh breeze
6	25–31	Strong breeze
7	32–38	Near gale
8	39–46	Gale
9	47–54	Strong gale
10	55–63	Storm
11	64–72	Violent storm
12	73+ over	Hurricane

Wave Height (in feet)	Effects at Sea		Effects on Land
–	Sea is like a mirror		Calm, smoke rises vertically
0–1	Ripple with appearance of scales		Wind direction indicated by smoke, but not wind vane
1–2	Small wavelets with smooth crests		Leaves rustle, wind felt on face, wind vane moves
2–3.5	Large wavelets, crests begin to break, scattered whitecaps		Leaves and twigs in constant motion, wind extends a light flag
3.5–6	Small waves becoming larger, numerous whitecaps		Wind raises dust and loose paper, small branches move
6–9	Moderate waves taking longer form, many whitecaps, some spray		Small trees move, smoke blown horizontal
9–13	Larger waves forming, whitecaps everywhere, more spray		Overhead wires whistle, umbrella is hard to hold
13–19	Sea heads up, white foam from breaking waves begins to be blown into streams		Whole trees sway, walking against wind is difficult
18–25	Moderately high waves of greater length, edges of crests begin to break into spindrift		Twigs break off trees, moving cars veer
23–32	High waves, sea begins to roll, dense streaks of foam, spray may begin to reduce visibility		Slight damage to buildings, shingles blown away
29–41	Very high waves with overhanging crests, sea takes a white appearance as foam is blown into very dense streaks, rolling is heavy and visibility is reduced		Trees uprooted, serious damage to buildings
37–52	Exceptionally high waves, sea covered with white foam patches, visibility is further reduced		Wide spread damage occurs, flying debris
46 and over	Air filled with foam, sea completely white with driving spray, visibility greatly reduced		Disaster, large debris becomes airborne

A SHORT HISTORY OF WIND POWER

The first use of wind to perform work did not appear in the form of a windmill but in sailing vessels that transported people, livestock, produce and other heavy cargo.

From Egypt to Persia and the Mediterranean: sailing and the first windmills

About 6,000 years ago a crowd of people gathered on the banks of the Nile River to witness a strange-looking contraption. It was probably the first time anyone had ever seen a ship move upstream using only the power of the wind. This ship had a large single rectangular sail hoisted on a mast. The mast could be rotated with ropes to turn the sail so it faced the wind at the correct angle to use the power of the wind to make the ship move.

For years before this, yoked oxen tethered to ropes had trudged slowly along a towpath that followed alongside the shore, pulling vessels loaded with cargo upstream against the current. It was a complicated and arduous task for both man and beast. The ability to harness the wind changed that.

It was not long before sailing vessels were moving up and down the Nile River carrying people, livestock and produce. This was the beginning of the age of sail. It would be 4,700 years before sails appeared on land to drive the first windmills in Persia.

The first Egyptian sailing vessels were small and likely constructed from bundled reeds, but these were soon replaced with a more durable wood-plank construction for use in much larger designs. These vessels had sails made from woven silk or cotton fabric.

By about 2000 B.C. the Arabs were using sail power to trade throughout the Persian Gulf, and by about 1200 B.C. the Greeks and Phoenicians had developed their own sailing vessels for trade in the Mediterranean.

Egyptian reed sailing vessel, 4000 B.C.

Egyptian sea-going ship, 1500 B.C. (top); early Roman trader, A.D. 20

Sailing vessels became the preferred way to transport heavy bulk goods to and from countries bordering the Mediterranean Sea. Traders who once used established land routes such as the Silk Road (so named because of the trade in silk from China) gradually switched to using sail power to transport people and goods by water once it became obvious that it was faster and cheaper. Using pack animals to pull loaded carts over land routes eventually became obsolete. The countries with the largest sailing fleets also became the wealthiest. By the first century A.D., sailing vessels were not only being used for trade but also for war, fishing and exploration.

It is probable that the common sight of square sails out on the water moving ships across the horizon inspired the first square-sailed windmills in Persia and Afghanistan around A.D. 700. These windmills were built on top of hills to make better use of the wind. They had a vertical axis — the axis being the center shaft around which the windmill turns — with horizontal spokes that supported sails made from slats of wood, animal hides or woven fabric. A gap in the surrounding brick and mud enclosure allowed the prevailing wind to enter on one side of the rotor to make it revolve. The other, returning side was sheltered from the wind by a wall.

These windmills were used for grinding grain, and they probably evolved first in drier regions where water was not readily available to power a water mill. Versions of these mills are still in use today in the more arid remote regions of Afghanistan. These mills can operate only when the wind is blowing from the right direction.

Sometime around the beginning of the second millennium, about 1,000 years ago, a new type of windmill appeared in countries bordering the eastern Mediterranean. These were *fixed mills*, such as the ones used on the Cyclades Islands, which were used to grind grain into flour and to scrape hair from animal hides, saving time and energy in what were tedious jobs that before then were done by hand. Unlike later mills, they did not have revolving tops that allowed them to be faced into the wind. Instead, they depended on prevailing winds to make them work.

Whoever first thought of using sails must have realized that attaching square or rectangular sails to the radiating spokes of a hub (the central place where they all join together, like the axle of a wheel) made no sense, since the overlap of the sails closer to the hub was a waste of material. A triangular sail would work much better if it was tied at two ends to the *spar* (the pole that holds the sail) on one side and the remaining free point fastened to the end of another spar radiating out from a second hub set further back on the axle. (See the photo of the Cyclades windmill on the next page.) This would allow the sail to be set at different angles to the wind. If the wind was blowing too hard, the speed could be controlled by *furling* — wrapping the sail around the leading spar to reduce the surface area exposed to the wind.

A Persian vertical axis windmill, A.D. 700. See also the photo at the top of page 32.

Fixed mills, Cyclades Islands (modern Greece), with sails partly furled.

In medieval times every farm on the island of Oeland, Sweden, had its own post mill.

A good idea spreads northward

The ingenious technology of the Cyclades windmills soon spread throughout the Mediterranean west to North Africa and north to Spain and then to France, England and Flanders (a medieval country which included modern-day Belgium and Holland).

There the idea was modified so that the body of the mill — known as "the buck" — could rotate around a single post. That change allowed the sails to be faced into the wind. Most of these *post mills* were built with four rectangular latticed wings to which cloth sails were attached. The sails could be furled to reduce them manually in strong winds and extended in light winds to harness maximum power. The earliest date on record of the post mill is 1191.

By the end of the 13th century, *tower mills* with a fixed, immovable stone masonry base came into common use. Only the wooden cap that was mounted on top of the tower had to be turned to face the sails into the wind. These windmills with high towers could carry much

longer sails, some almost touching the ground, and were aptly called "ground-sailers."

Dutch windmills are probably the most widely recognized worldwide. Much of the Netherlands is below sea level and consists of flat reclaimed land. If water is not continuously

A tower mill in southern Spain. The long pole was used to rotate the cap at the top.

pumped out of canals and lower areas it would once again become submerged. Large windmills called polder mills were built and equipped to scoop water from lakes and other wet areas into drainage ditches, thereby creating dry land.

In the early 17th century, investors formed a company to drain Lake Beemster, north of Amsterdam. At first they thought that 16 windmills would be enough, but in the end 50 windmills were needed to keep the land from flooding. That land soon became valuable real estate. In 1999, almost 400 years later, the Beemster Polder was designated a World Heritage Site.

In the past the polder mill was the only way to keep up with the constant seepage of water. Now automatic electric and diesel pumps handle most of the pumping; however, there are still many windmills at work to perform this vital task.

On a smaller scale, the tjasker was used to pump water from agricultural land. This small device was perfect for keeping water from flooding planted fields. It used the wind to turn the rotor and drive an Archimedean screw, which slowly draws water up a short distance and into a drainage ditch.

A tjasker, a small wind-powered pump; (below) Dutch windmills along a canal in Zaandam, Netherlands, circa 1880.

The Industrial Revolution

Early inventions of the Industrial Revolution included some strange-looking windmills that tried to optimize the power of wind. The oddest-looking one was the windmill Ernest Bollée built almost entirely from steel components constructed in France in 1868. It was used for pumping water. Only 313 were ever built. By 1914, 300 Éoliennes Bollée were in operation across France. Today 78 remain and a historical society is dedicated to the restoration of these very finely built curiosities. The look and concept of this windmill may have influenced the development of the American wind pump.

All of the many innovations used to improve the windmill so it could perform to its maximum mechanical potential for grinding grain, pumping water or sawing lumber were an important part of the beginning of the

A windmill with fantail; (right) the rotor of the Éolienne Bollée at Roueïre, France (1898).

500 years to perfect the windmill

From about 1100 to 1600, windmill mechanics and sails evolved as new inventions were introduced to improve efficiency and automation. Devices such as the fantail attached at the rear of the cap at the top of the tower automatically turned the sails to face the wind. *Spring sails* made from connected slats of wood could be opened or closed manually and fitted with springs, which allowed the slats to open in a violent gust of wind preventing damage to the sails. The *self-furling sail*, a brilliant invention, allowed the sails to be adjusted while still in motion. The aerodynamic shaping of the *leading edge* of the sails would later be used in aircraft design.

Industrial Revolution. However, the steam engine and the internal combustion engine soon made the windmill obsolete for many applications. Just as sailing ships were replaced with steam ships, noisy, exhaust-spewing engines fouled the air as many windmills fell out of use and into ruins. Eventually, when electricity and the power-line *grid* came into common use, the need for windmills declined even further. Anyone could switch on a machine to perform work anywhere anytime.

Pumping water for livestock in America

When the first Europeans arrived in New England they found abundant rivers and streams to power their mills, so very few windmills were built to grind grain or saw lumber. As the frontier expanded, pioneers travelled westward to settle on prairie land. The new "sod busters" and ranchers found much drier conditions. Wells and ponds were dug to provide water for cattle and other livestock. Many of these ponds dried up during the summer months, leaving only the wells with hand pumps to supply water. When cattle-grazing operations expanded into regions with sparse vegetation, huge tracts of land were required to feed large herds. Available water was the only limiting factor. A solution came in 1854 with the self-regulating wind pump invented by Daniel Halladay.

These windmills were designed to operate in very light breezes and made small and strong enough to withstand the sudden violent winds of prairie storms. The closely set blades take maximum advantage of the wind passing through their *circle of rotation*. The center part of the fan is open to allow less effective wind to pass through and to create less resistance in high wind conditions.

Early models had wood blades and towers that were eventually replaced with more durable

An American wind pump still provides water for cattle.

steel construction. A 6-foot-diameter rotor wind pump could pump up to 180 gallons per hour in a 15-to-20-mph wind. The only maintenance required was to change the oil in the gearbox once a year. By 1930 there were 600,000 of this type of windmill in operation on farms and ranches across America.

Many of these windmills, with brand names like Ace, Aermotor, Buckeye, Daisy, Dandy, Eclipse, Fountain, Steel Queen, and Sunflower, are still in operation today. They have become an icon of the rural way of life in North America.

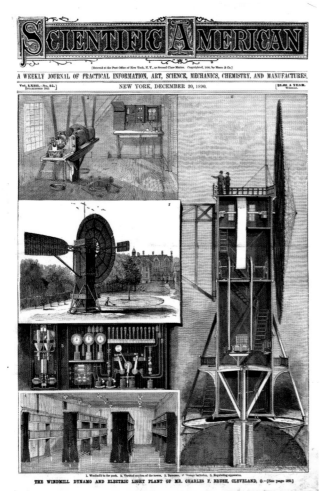

SCIENTIFIC AMERICAN

[Entered at the Post Office of New York, N. Y., as Second Class Matter. Copyrighted, 1890, by Munn & Co.]

A WEEKLY JOURNAL OF PRACTICAL INFORMATION, ART, SCIENCE, MECHANICS, CHEMISTRY, AND MANUFACTURES.

Vol. LXIII.—No. 25.
[Established 1845.]

NEW YORK, DECEMBER 20, 1890.

[$3.00 A YEAR.
WEEKLY.]

1. Windmill in the park. 2. Vertical section of the tower. 3. Dynamo. 4. Storage batteries. 5. Regulating apparatus.

THE WINDMILL DYNAMO AND ELECTRIC LIGHT PLANT OF MR. CHARLES F. BRUSH, CLEVELAND, O.—[See page 389.]

Scientific American magazine featured the Charles F. Brush wind generator, built in Cleveland, Ohio, in 1888.

Generating electricity

Today, anyone who knows anything about wind power knows that it can be used to generate electricity. In 1888 Charles F. Brush, inventor of the arc light, created the first wind-powered electrical generator in America, a remarkable achievement considering how new electricity was for the general public. At the time, hydro or water power was the only energy source considered feasible for generating electricity. The rotor was 58 feet in diameter and the structure could rotate 360 degrees to face into the wind.

In Vermont in 1941, on a 2,000-foot summit called Grandpa's Knob, a huge wind turbine was slowly assembled on a 110-foot tower. Built by Smith and Putnam, this 240-ton structure was the first wind-powered generator to produce over 1 megawatt of electricity. The twin blades withstood high winds but a main bearing failure caused one of the 75-foot blades to snap off, sending it 700 feet down the mountain slope.

The Smith and Putnam wind turbine at Grandpa's Knob, Vermont, in 1941.

EXPERIMENTING WITH ELECTRICITY

After experimenting with some of the projects in this book you might like to try to generate enough power to light a light-emitting diode (an LED) or small light bulb. The contraption shown at right is only an example of where such exploration might lead you — there is no detailed step-by-step description of how to assemble this particular project. That would take another entire book to explain.

Moreover, to generate any amount of useable or reliable electricity we would never recommend starting with a paper or fabric sail windmill. Anyone starting from scratch to build an entire system would have to consider many factors such as end use, limit of materials, wind zones, transmission resistance limits, permanent magnet alternators, gearing, noise and safety. It is almost a daunting task to begin.

Thus forewarned, here are a few suggestions. Small servo motors can be salvaged from broken ink jet printers, computers fans or obsolete disc drives. Rather than feeding power into the motor to make it turn, you can use the two wires to attach an LED. Flick the main shaft of the motor to discover which direction it must turn to generate electricity.

The next step would be to determine how fast the motor must spin by using some kind of gearing or pulley device, as most windmills don't rotate fast enough to apply a direct drive system. This is where you will have to concentrate most of your experimenting time, collecting rubber belts, O-rings or appropriate gears. If you look closely at the photograph you can see how the simple metal bracket can be adjusted up or down to accommodate the length of a belt by repositioning a single screw. For larger windmills it may be necessary to use bearings on the main shaft to reduce friction.

For this experiment with a four-sail windmill, a servo motor of unknown origin and power output was used. The rotation of the motor was in the wrong direction. And the pulley broke in the wild winds in which it was tested.

Certainly there was enough power from the sails to light the LED, but based on this one attempt, there was not enough evidence to suggest any expected outcome. Further experimentation would be needed to determine what particular motor, sail area, circle of rotation size, wind speed and gearing would make it work. In other words, you can use the example shown here as a basis for your own experimentation, but do not try to copy it exactly and expect that you will then success-fully power a light bulb!

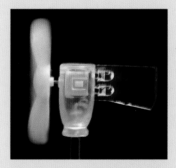

You can buy ready-made micro wind-powered light kits such as the educational toy shown here, but with some thought, ambition and patience, plus a supply of found objects and materials around your house and garage, you might surprise yourself. All good results are achieved by solving one problem at a time.

Marcellus Jacobs with one of his model turbines.

Common sense and the Jacobs wind turbine

From 1927 to 1957 the Jacobs Wind Electric Company, Minneapolis, manufactured 20,000 commercial wind turbines producing 1.8 kilowatts (kW), 2.5 kW, and 3.0 kW of power that were sold to generate electricity on remote farms, ranches, commercial utility and government sites.

Using common sense, brothers Marcellus and Joseph Jacobs developed these well-built turbines through trial and error prototypes. Their experiments with different blade shapes and different numbers of blades led to their discovery that using three blades would maximize wind efficiency and minimize the vibration that was characteristic of two-blade designs. This three-blade configuration is in common use today on all large wind-farm turbines around the world. To keep the rotors from going into *overspeed* and inevitable self-destruction, Jacobs devised a regulator on the hub that would rotate the blade away from the wind to maintain a steady, maximum revolutions per minute (rpm) even in storm conditions.

While developing their wind turbines, Jacobs filed 19 patents (of their total of 68 patents) that solved a wide scope of problems ranging from blade shape to generator construction. Their wind turbines gained a great reputation for durability. A Jacobs wind turbine was used by Admiral Byrd on his expedition to the South Pole in the early 1930s and was still spinning in the wind 25 years later.

If NASA had paid more attention to the innovative technologies developed by Jacobs in the 1930s it is doubtful they would have used a vibration-prone two-blade design for all of their Mod series of experimental wind generators developed in the 1970s.

The Gedser Mollen was built in Denmark in 1957 and provided electric power for 11 years.

The Gedser Mollen

Johannes Juul, a Danish engineer with experience in aircraft, had a 200 kW wind turbine built on the southern coast of Denmark near Gedser. It was the first wind turbine with an asynchronous AC generator connected to an electrical grid. It ran for 11 years before being decommissioned. The three aerodynamic blade tips, through centrifugal force, could turn 90 degrees — thereby preventing the rotor from going into destructive overspeed.

NASA and beyond

From 1974 to 1981 NASA's Research Center at Plum Brook Station in Sandusky, Ohio, built 13 experimental horizontal axis wind turbines. Four sizes — 200 kW, 2 megawatts (mW), 2.5 mW, and 3.5 mW — were tested. Most of these designs used two-blade propeller-type rotors. NASA engineers Larry Viterna and Bob Corrigan ran extensive tests to determine the efficiency of wind turbine blades in strong wind conditions. Data from this research is still used today to determine the best blade shape, pitch (angle) and speed limits for wind turbines.

The Mod 0 used a single blade for tests. The Mod 1 wind turbine with a downwind propeller had to be shut down because of the intense low-frequency noise that it produced. The NASA Mod 5a turbine installed in Oahu, Hawaii, is still in use today producing 3.4 mW of electricity.

Three NASA Mod 2 turbines, each generating 2.5 mW, at Goodnoe Hills, Washington, in 1981.

› SOME BASIC PRINCIPLES

Sailboats and windmills

As a sailboat moves across an open body of water, its sails are constantly moving into new undisturbed wind. As a stationary windmill's sails spin in a circle of rotation, each sail, or blade, leaves behind in its *wake* some disturbed, turbulent air that can hinder the performance of the following sail. As long as the sails turn slowly, this *fouling* effect is not a problem, but as the sails increase in speed there is less time for the turbulent air to pass through the circle of rotation. This can limit the speed at which the rotor can turn. The effect on each sail can be seen as the rotor that powers the rotation reaches maximum speed. The sails lose their initial efficient shape and start to *luff*, meaning that they flap back and forth, because the fouled air is being pushed out of the way before it can pass through the gap between the sails.

If a work *load* is applied to the main shaft of the windmill (for instance, by engaging the gears to turn a millstone), a slow and steady rotation speed can be achieved and the sails will retain their efficient shape. If the load is removed from the main shaft, the rotor and sails will go into *overspeed* and the sails will loose their efficient shape and begin to luff. Damage to the spars and sails can result if the rotor is allowed to go into overspeed. Sailboats do not have this fouling or overspeed problem because there is a heavy constant load or resistance because of the weight of the sailboat being pulled through the water.

This six-sail windmill stood up well as long as sufficient load was applied to the main shaft. However, once the load was removed, the sails flew off and got tangled in the stays (the strings that hold the structure together).

Windmills with sails

When you look at a sailboat moving through the water on a set course with the sails trimmed for maximum performance, you will notice the sails billow out and hold their shape. The drag or resistance of the boat through the water will never allow the boat to reach a speed that is the same as the speed of the wind. This is also true with sails on a windmill as long as there is a load applied to the main shaft to slow it down. In the following photos you can see what happens when there is not a load applied to the main shaft.

The six-sail windmill in the photo below performed well when a sufficient load was applied to the main shaft. (Load — the weight of an opposing force — was applied by hand at the back end of the main shaft.)

When the wind increased in speed, three of the sails were removed to reduce pressure on the rotor. When the load on the main shaft was removed, the sails flew off and tangled in the stays.

In this first photo of a four-sail windmill, the wind has increased in speed. The bottom and right sails have held their form as the rotor turns but the top sail and left sail do not have enough pressure from the wind to overcome the resistance on the back of the sails as they turn. They make a flapping sound as they luff back and forth.

As the rotor increases speed (second photo), all the sails begin to luff.

In a sudden gust of wind, the rotor goes into overspeed and the sails flap wildly. This (third photo) was the point just before the lower right sail detached itself from the back spar. This would not have happened if some resistance had been applied to the main shaft.

However, in slowing down the rotor, another problem occurs. If the rotor can't spin fast enough to relieve the wind pressure, the supporting spars may break. The only way to correct this situation would be to reduce the surface of the sails by reefing them in (wrapping them around the leading spar).

This is the main reason why windmills with sails are not widely used to generate electricity. They have to be constantly adjusted for wind conditions, and if for some reason the gear on the main shaft becomes disengaged, the rotor will destroy itself when it goes into overspeed.

Building a windmill with cloth sails will help you to understand the problems controlling the speed and stresses from the wind when so much surface area is used to turn a rotor.

However, this kind of project is very time consuming and requires advanced skill and tools, all to make something that can be destroyed very easily. Make sure you have some way of reducing the size of sails and some way of putting a load on the main shaft to slow it down.

Angle of attack

For a sailboat to move through the water it must have its sails set at the correct angle. If the sails are not set at the correct angle to the wind, the sailboat will not move efficiently through the water. A sailboat also has a rudder to keep it on course and a keel to prevent it from drifting sideways, but it is the sails, when set properly, that use the power of the wind to make the sailboat move.

The following diagram shows how the sails must be set for the sailboat to move in different directions: angle into the wind, across the wind and downwind.

Sails on a sailboat luff when the wind changes intensity or direction. If a sudden gust of wind arises, the sails must be let out, or loosened, to spill the excess wind. When the sails are let out, they will luff or flap violently. Failing to let the sails out could result in the boat capsizing.

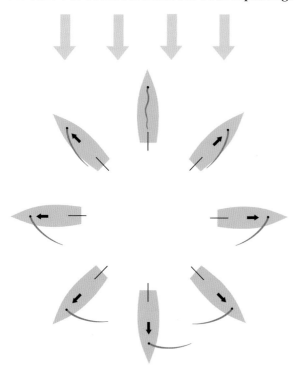

The sails must be set at different angles to the wind, depending on the direction of the wind and the direction in which the boat is trying to travel.

When the wind dies down to a reasonable strength, the sails can once again be trimmed. This is done by hauling the sails in just to the point where they no longer luff. It is at this point that the sails are set to their maximum efficiency.

If the wind increases in strength it may become necessary to reduce the area of a sail exposed to the wind by reefing or by furling, different methods of tying or winding up the sail to make it smaller. In gale conditions a storm sail, which is much smaller, is used to keep the sailboat from capsizing. Another way to prevent a sailboat from capsizing is to turn it so the bow is facing into the wind, thereby changing the angle of the sails so that the wind can more easily pass by.

Similarly early windmills were equipped with sails that could be furled to reduce sail area in windy conditions. In storm conditions the best practice was to remove the sails and turn the rotor sideways to the direction of the wind to prevent damage. Most windmills were designed to operate in lighter winds. Not until spring sails were invented was there a way to prevent sudden gusts of wind from damaging the rotors. Because windmills are fixed permanently to one spot and cannot heel over like a sailboat they are more prone to damage.

For the sails on a windmill to work properly, the plane of rotation must face directly into the wind (at a 90-degree angle of attack) taking the full force head on.

Early windmills had no way of changing the pitch or angle of the sails to reduce wind pressure. This had to be done manually by furling the sails. On modern wind turbines the blades can automatically change pitch in high winds to reduce stress on the blades and prevent them from bending and from going into overspeed. These are called variable-pitch blades.

A sailboat passes a windmill on the Norfolk Broads, United Kingdom.

You can see how blade pitch affects the speed of the rotor in low and high wind conditions in the project section by building the variable-pitch windmill (X Windmill A), at page 56.

Streamlining

The body shapes of sailboat hulls, ships, canoes and submarines mimic the shapes of fish, porpoises and whales. Rudders, keels and paddles function much like fins, tails and flukes because the streamlined shapes allow

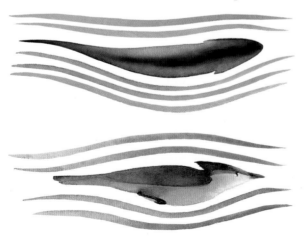

them to work efficiently in fluid water by minimizing turbulence and resistance, or *drag*.

Similarly the body shapes of aircraft are streamlined like the bodies of birds, and aircraft wings are intentionally shaped like the wings of birds to allow them to pass through fluid air with minimum resistance.

Airfoils, lift and drag

A closer look at a cross-section of a bird wing reveals the same airfoil shape of an aircraft wing. The elliptically rounded leading edge of each kind of wing, natural and manmade, separates the passing air stream in two, minimizing turbulence and resistance. The *camber* (curvature from leading edge to *trailing edge*) causes the passing air over the top surface to move faster (it has a greater distance to travel), creating lower pressure. Air passing more slowly over the surface on the under side (it has less distance to travel) creates high pressure. The result is that there is an upward force on the wing called *lift*. Lift is the force on a surface that is perpendicular to the oncoming flow. Drag is the parallel force in opposition to the oncoming flow.

Bernoulli's Principle

The concept of lift from pressure differentials was first expressed in *Hydrodynamica* in 1738 by the Dutch-Swiss mathematician Daniel Bernoulli. A simplified version of Bernoulli's Principle can be stated as this: a fluid (such as air or water) moving over a surface creates a force (lift) perpendicular to the direction of flow.

To demonstrate this, take a piece of paper and blow across the top surface. The result is that the limp paper will rise. Another example is with a ping-pong ball and a funnel. Place the ping-pong ball into the wide opening of the funnel and blow through the small end. The unexpected occurs when the ball does not fly out of the funnel but is held in place by the passing air. The funnel can be turned upside down and the ball seems to defy gravity.

The suction effect of this principle is apparent when you blow across the opening of a tube placed in water. The harder you blow, the higher the water rises in the tube.

The lift factor when applied to an ice-sailing or land-sailing vehicle (where there is very little friction) will allow the vehicle to travel faster than the speed of the wind. This is also true for windmills and wind turbines, since they have very little resistance to turn unless there is a load applied such as turning a millstone or spinning a generator.

Lift can be lessened by the surface that the air is passing over if it is irregular and causes turbulence and drag. A good example of this is when ice forms on an airplane wing due to weather conditions: the result is less lift with added weight and that can cause the airplane to crash.

An airfoil is the shape of a wing (or blade or sail) seen in cross-section. Airfoils come in many shapes, all designed to increase lift and decrease drag. Air speed and lift requirements are taken into account when an airfoil is designed. A model of any proposed design is first tested in a wind tunnel to make sure that it will perform to expectations. A wing airfoil for a heavy equipment transport aircraft requires more lift than a wing for a supersonic jet. On the next page are cross-section profiles for wings of various aircraft.

Airfoils and wind turbines

Large wind turbine blades travel in a circle of rotation around a single axis. This path is different from the path of a sailboat or an airplane, both of which travel in a straight line and are constantly exposed to passing undisturbed air. A wind turbine rotor will slow down if a blade has to pass through the wake (disturbed air) of the blade ahead of it. There must be enough space between blades

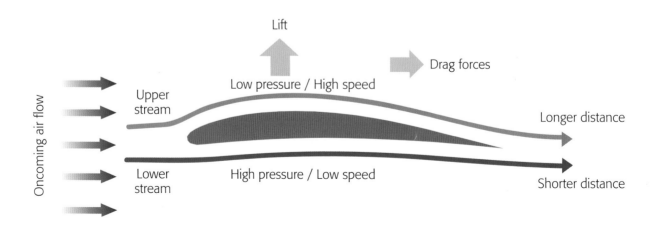

Lift

Drag forces

Low pressure / High speed

Upper stream

Oncoming air flow

Longer distance

Lower stream

High pressure / Low speed

Shorter distance

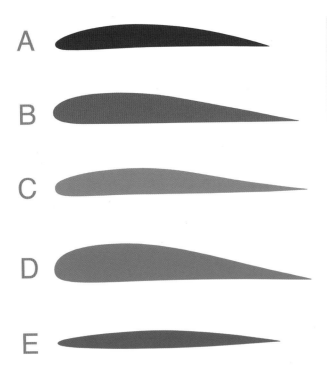

A
B
C
D
E

(A) single prop airplane; (B) jet airliner;
(C) stable flying wing; (D) heavy load transport;
(E) supersonic jet

to allow turbulent air to pass by before the next blade arrives. This is why the airfoil shape of these highly engineered blades is so critical for maximum performance.

If you look at a typical wind turbine blade you can see that it is not as consistent in cross-section as a wing of an airplane. The whole of an airplane wing travels through the air at the same speed. This is not true of a wind turbine blade, where the part of the blade closest to the hub or axis moves very slowly compared to the tips of the blade — which can reach speeds of 150 mph. The further away from the hub, the more aerodynamic the shape must be so that it does not create unnecessary turbulence in its wake.

The blade of a modern wind turbine is tapered to create a more aerodynamic shape.

›LIMITATIONS

Betz's Law

There are limits to how much energy can be extracted from wind.

If we look at any size circle of rotation of a *rotor* (the area within the circle in which the hub and blades spin), we are limited to the volume of air that passes through it. Larger rotors, because they have larger circles of rotation and can capture more air, have the potential for producing greater power than smaller rotors. How we capture that passing air and convert it to power depends on the design of the device operating in that circle.

The blades of a wind turbine redirect the flow of the wind. They cannot capture all the force of the wind because they must allow at least some of the air to pass through. However, if there was no space between the blades, they would simply block all of the flow of wind. The wind would exert a pressure only on the surface blocking the continuous flow; the rotor would not turn or transmit any useable power to a generator. In all cases, to make a rotor spin, we must partially block the flow of air by deflecting it but still allowing some of it to pass through the circle of rotation. This can be done in many ways and will depend on the expectations for any given design.

For example, a farm wind pump may block more air than a wind turbine used to generate electricity. The expectations for a farm wind pump are to operate in very light breezes to pump water but also to be able to withstand high winds without blowing over. That is why its rotors seldom exceed 8 feet in diameter. The angle of the blades are set so that in high winds, after reaching maximum speed, the back of the moving blades start to push air and thereby cause a force against the direction of rotation. This keeps the blade from going into overspeed and flying apart from extreme centrifugal force.

All windmills and wind turbines are limited by what is called Betz's Law. This states that it is only possible to capture 59.6 percent of the energy in the wind, which is the best compromise between blocking the wind entirely or allowing it all to pass. This is the compromise any wind device must make, whether it is a farm water pump or a huge wind turbine built to generate electricity.

Hurricane winds

The greatest threat to any windmill or wind turbine is too much wind. If the rotor is allowed to increase in speed to the point where it is said to go into overspeed (out of control), the

Wind turbine blade tip brakes turn 90 degrees to the plane of rotation to help control the speed of the rotor and prevent damage to the blades and tower.

forces on the flexible blades may cause them to hit the support tower, the centrifugal force may cause a rotor to fly off, the *torque* on the main shaft bearings may cause them to fail, or the speed of the blades passing through turbulent air may cause the whole structure to break apart or blow over.

Various devices on modern turbines prevent them from going into overspeed. A tip brake is commonly used on each blade. This is a short section on the end of each blade that deploys when the centrifugal force of the spinning blade reaches a maximum speed; the brake allows the tip to turn 90 degrees to the plane of rotation. This has the effect of slowing the rotor.

Another method of controlling rotor speed is the use of variable-pitch blades: these turn away from the oncoming wind to reduce exposed surface area and to increase drag. In extreme conditions a computer will turn the rotor sideways into the wind to prevent

damage. Modern wind turbines must use more than one safety device to ensure survival in extreme conditions in case one system fails.

Turbulence

When moving air encounters an obstacle, it is fluid enough to flow around it. If the obstacle is aerodynamically streamlined, the moving air separates to flow around the obstacle and continues once past the object with very little disturbance to the flow lines. On the other hand, when wind blows against a flat surface it is forced to escape in all directions, causing many vortices (rotating swirls) of disturbance in the flow. This is called *turbulence.*

An example of this is demonstrated when a paddle is drawn through the water to propel a canoe. The result is many little eddies left behind in the water after the stroke has finished. This prolonged disturbance is similar to the flow of air around a blunt object. If the paddle

When wind blows against a flat surface it is forced to escape in all directions, causing disturbances in the flow of air called turbulence. Houses and topographical features such as hills can cause turbulence, so wind turbines must be built as high as possible away from these surface irregularities.

Open-water wind farms, where the wind can be "cleaner" and also stronger, are a good alternative to large land-based operations.

is used as a rudder in the passing water, so that the blade's narrow edge instead of its flat face is the shape that meets the flow of water, there is very little resistance and very little turbulence produced.

Topographical features such as hills and large buildings can create turbulence in wind. This is why modern wind turbines need to operate as high as possible on towers where there is very little turbulence from ground surface irregularities. Turbulence can put an uneven load on each blade as the rotor turns, causing resistance resulting in a loss of power and creating unwanted stress and vibration. Blades passing through the lowest section of the circle are more prone to ground-level turbulence and the disturbed air passing around the tower itself. To avoid tower- induced turbulence, many rotors are tilted slightly upwards so the moving blades avoid the disturbed air near the tower.

As a blade passes the tower it can produce a low-frequency pulse that can be heard as far away as a mile. Any noise produced by a wind turbine is a sign of inefficiency. The challenge for engineers is to produce quieter wind turbines. The quieter they are, the more efficient they are in harnessing the power of the wind.

Pulse and vibration

When NASA developed their Mod series experimental wind turbines in the 1980s, they were surprised to find that the extra-sturdy towers that supported the downwind rotors caused horrific noise problems in the form of a low-frequency pulse, often described as a "thump," as each blade passed through a wind dead zone behind the tower. Complaints from surrounding residents resulted in NASA having to shut it down.

It should be noted that almost all large modern wind turbines have rotors that face upwind from the tower and require controls to keep them pointed in the right direction. This solves some of the noise problems but there is still an envelope of disturbed air in front of the tower that the blades must pass through, creating some low-frequency noise.

Why don't we build wind turbines on our homes or barns or even tall office buildings? Retrofitting a building with a wind turbine is a very bad idea. Any wind turbine has to be firmly mounted to resist wind loads. If it is mounted to the top of a high building it will transmit any noise to every part of the rigid structure. Efforts to try this have failed because of pulse and vibration noise; the result is always the wind turbines being dismantled.

Wind farms — which can contain as few as four or as many as a hundred or more turbines — built close to populated areas have caused endless problems with noise. The noise is both of a low frequency from rotor blades and of a higher frequency from the gears and generators. Some residents living near wind farms describe the incessant noise as relentless torture. Many complain of sleepless nights, headaches and other medical problems. The issue for them is regulated setback minimums. Currently these setbacks are inadequate to protect the public. It has been suggested that large turbines should not be any closer than 2 kilometers (a little more than a mile) from any residence. Placing wind farms out in open water, where there is stronger and "cleaner" wind, is seen as a good solution to both noise and turbulent wind problems.

A question of size

The costs of installing a wind turbine may be offset by how much money the turbine can make in the sale of the electricity that it generates. Currently in North America it costs approximately $40,000 to install a 10 kW single-household wind turbine. That price includes the nacelle, tower installation, generator and the necessary electronics. This is more than most individual households would be willing to pay but it does not produce enough power to make money for any wind energy developer.

Where only one turbine is to be erected it does not make economic sense to install a small turbine as the payback period for the initial investment would be too long. The trend is to build larger and larger turbines to offset the high costs of installation. More effort is needed to develop cost-effective micro wind devices.

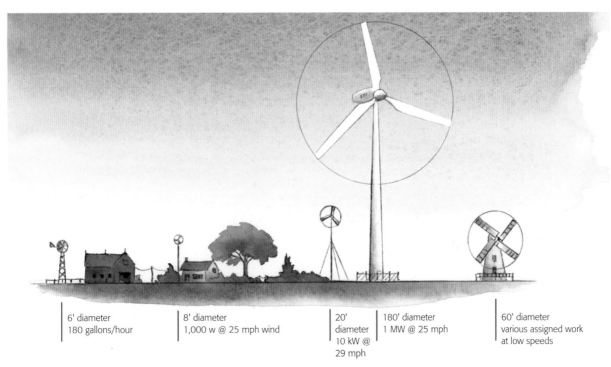

| 6' diameter | 8' diameter | 20' diameter | 180' diameter | 60' diameter |
| 180 gallons/hour | 1,000 w @ 25 mph wind | 10 kW @ 29 mph | 1 MW @ 25 mph | various assigned work at low speeds |

This diagram illustrates the diameter of sweep for various rotors and the corresponding power outputs of each. It is apparent that a slight increase in size produces substantially more power. This is why most wind energy developers' economic philosophy is "bigger is better."

›HAWTS VERSUS VAWTS

There are two main kinds of wind turbines: HAWTs and VAWTs.

The main axis or shaft of a HAWT (horizontal axis wind turbine) is horizontal. The blades are joined in the center to a hub and rotate in a circle that is perpendicular to the ground, as in the original Dutch windmills. The main axis of a VAWT (vertical axis turbine) is vertical, which means that the blades rotate around the shaft horizontally, as in the first Persian windmills.

HAWTs are primarily used to generate large amounts of electricity to feed the power grid for communities. Wind is harnessed most efficiently using the large sweep area of these types of wind turbines. They have very little drag to slow them down. But they need special controls to turn them into the wind because they work better that way.

VAWTs are best suited to low power-output requirements. They produce less noise and do not need to be turned into the wind, but are subject to much greater drag on the side of the rotor returning into the wind so they produce less electricity.

VAWTs spin at higher rpm but slow down very significantly when a load is applied in the form of a generator. This type of wind turbine has generally been abandoned for generating electricity to feed the grid. They are best suited for extra or backup power to charge batteries, for outdoor ambient lighting, or for use in remote off-grid areas where frequent service is not possible, such as for open-water light buoys and weather stations.

Ancient and modern examples of vertical axis wind turbines: the photograph at top is from Nashtifan, the ancient Persian city of windmills.

The main axis of a HAWT (horizontal axis wind turbine) is horizontal, as in the original Dutch windmills. The blades rotate in a circle perpendicular to the ground.

The main axis of a VAWT (vertical axis wind turbine) is vertical. The blades rotate around the shaft horizontally, as in the first Persian windmills.

HAWTs PROs	VAWTs PROs
› Sweep areas are larger › Better for high power generation › Variable-pitch blades allow for optimum angle of attack to the wind, allowing for more efficient output in varying conditions	› Can operate and start up in lower wind speeds › Don't have to be faced into the wind › Generators and other components are at ground level › Can accommodate ground-level winds and turbulence as well as funneled wind › Produce less noise
HAWTs CONs	**VAWTs CONs**
› Rotors need to be faced into the wind as it changes › Heavy generators, gears, brakes and electronics need to be on top of tower, making repairs and maintenance more difficult › Transportation of huge components is costly and difficult › Noise issues as yet unresolved	› Create more drag on rotor as one side returns into the wind › Require guy wires for support › Produce less power than HAWTs and should probably only be used where high output is not expected › Weight of entire structure rests on top of generator, making it necessary to dismantle for repairs

EXPERIMENTING WITH WIND

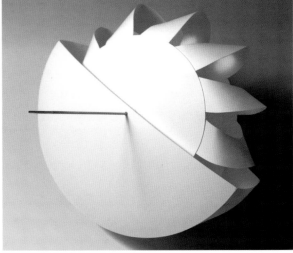

You can choose how you wish to work through the projects in this book. If you are not sure what you are doing, begin by following the simple directions for the first few pinwheels and the Easy 6-Blade VAWT, then try a more difficult project after you get a feel for cutting and shaping paper.

Younger readers may have to seek help for some projects, especially where special care, dexterity or strength with a sharp knife, power drill or other advanced tools is needed.

The directions for each project are shown in graphic sequence. Not all of the steps in the advanced projects are spelled out in detail. This is to encourage you to try to find your own solutions to the problems you may encounter, and to experiment with different materials, shapes and construction techniques. The photographs will give you plenty of information if you study them carefully. All dimensions are approximate and can be changed.

This book should be regarded as only an introduction into experimenting with wind devices. Once you feel comfortable with the geometry, materials and construction, pursue

The shield on this prototype had the effect of fouling the air inside the shield. It might be better used as a ventilator rather than to generate electricity. The paper warped and rubbed on the inside of the shield.

your own direction and try developing your own ideas.

Pictured on this page are two of the projects I tried and discarded. They are crude prototypes that were tested to see if there was any potential in the design. I like them very much for their sculptural form but they are quite useless when tested in the wind. They did not take very long to make, but were the basis for trying something else.

Drawing

The first step is to draw your project. Sketches save time because you don't have to construct anything. When you have a sketch that looks promising, then you can make a crude prototype to see if it works. Using a compass, ruler and pencil you can draw hundreds of different rotor designs. At right are some sample drawings to give you an idea of how to develop a design on paper.

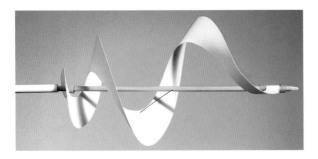

This spiral-shaped rotor works well but is too difficult to balance. It is more appropriate for a toy.

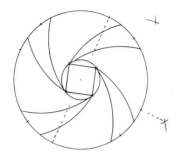

These are concept drawings that were created using only a pencil, ruler and a compass.

Try to figure out how each drawing could be cut and *scored* to produce a working windmill, then try drawing your own concept drawings using these simple tools. You will have a better idea what the lines on the drawing mean after you read the instructions for the simpler projects in this book.

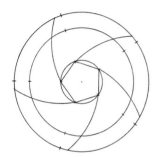

Keep in mind you will need a hub to which the blades must be attached. A square hub will have 2 or 4 blades. A hexagonal hub will have 3 or 6 blades.

For balance the blades must be equal in size, equal distance apart and concentric (have the same center).

The blades will have to be angled so they are turned into the wind when bent along the score lines in order for it to work properly. A gap between each of the blades will allow air to pass through more easily and allow the *rotor* to turn efficiently in the wind.

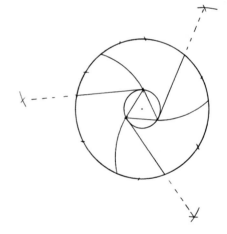

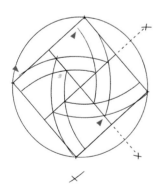

Note: The red arrows point to minor errors in drawing. At this stage there is no need for perfection. Save the accuracy for the final working prototype. Spend the time to figure out what the shape of the blades will be, whether or not there will be a gap between the blades, and where to score the paper.

Prototypes

Use inexpensive paper, a glue gun, staples, tape, double-sided tape, white glue, elastic bands, and any other recycled material to make a prototype. The finished prototype has to be good enough only to use as an experiment to see if it might actually work. If it works, you can take the time to build a better version later. This is key to experimentation.

Materials

Papers and cardboard

Ordinary paper is the least expensive material to use for making experimental wind devices. If you are unsure of what you are doing, make a prototype from any lightweight bond paper first to see if your concept will work. Before you use more expensive papers such as hot press watercolor paper, make your pinwheel from card stock or Bristol board. You can even use cardboard recycled from cereal boxes. Starting over again or making mistakes won't become costly.

Easy-to-cut and inexpensive 8-by-11-inch card stock is recommended for prototype construction. The chart below lists various papers and their properties.

It may be necessary to use stiffer material in cases where you don't want the pieces to bend or change shape. In that case, use a stiff 2-ply or 3-ply cardboard. Corrugated cardboard box material will also stay flat and not change shape. See the note on cutting cardboard later on this page. If you already have some paper or cardboard that you think might work, test it first to see if it has the properties you need. Check to see if it possible to cut and or shape with the tools you have at hand.

Other useful objects

Long hardened steel pins; small smooth glass, plastic or wood beads; straight steel wire and thin steel rod for axles; several lengths of square-profile softwood (3 feet of 1/4 inch by 1/4 inch); small glue gun; white paper glue and wood glue.

Tools

At right is a list of basic and inexpensive tools you will find useful. Also handy would be a small fine-toothed saw and a pair of needlenose pliers for bending wire. A power drill may be needed to drill holes for dowels and axles.

Cutting tools and cutting surfaces

Cutting tools should be sharp; the sharper they are, the smoother and cleaner your cuts will be. You will need scissors, toe-nail scissors with curved blades, a small utility knife with snap-off sections or a scalpel with a straight cutting edge, and a soft plastic cutting surface or a smooth piece of plywood.

Note: One of the hardest materials to work with is 2- or 3-ply cardboard. It is not easy to cut a curve from this material and assistance may be required. Use a cutting board and a sharp knife like an X-acto knife, a scalpel with a straight cutting edge, or a small utility knife.

PAPERS AND CARDBOARDS

	Watercolor paper 90 or 120 lb hot press	Card stock, Bristol board	Cereal box cardboard
Made from	Cotton fiber	Wood fiber	Recycled wood fiber
Properties	Stiff but flexible, strong, scores well, long lasting, curled pieces hold shape	Softer than cotton fiber, curled pieces don't hold shapes for long periods of time	Prone to kinks and surface cracking, requires careful handling, printed side can be spray-painted in one coat, blank inside good for drawing, printed side does not glue well
Cost	Expensive	Economical	Free
Good for	Finished work	Experimental prototypes	Painted finished work, pinwheels, but not other curled pieces

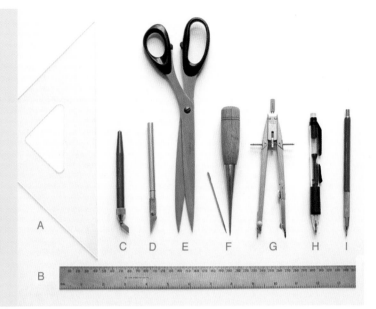

BASIC TOOLS

A   Transparent ruler or set square for drawing straight lines (Do *not* use for cutting)

B   Steel ruler for cutting straight lines

C   Swivel knife for cutting curved lines

D   X-acto knife

E   Long sharp scissors

F   Large needle or awl

G   Compass

H   Fine HB graphite mechanical drafting pencil (0.5)

I   Steel mechanical drafting pencil with a small nail with rounded point for scoring

Drawing tools

You will need a compass with sharp lead and a sharp metal tip, sharpened pencils (HB, H, B) and a metal ruler or ruler with a steel edge. A set square is useful for drawing right angles.

Use the kind of compass that has the pencil built in: this compass has a chisel-shaped graphite tip. To draw a circle or part of a circle, apply constant pressure at point C while rotating the compass with the graphite tip lightly touching the paper. This will produce a fine but visible circle line. (If you can't get this kind of compass, you can use one with a screw-on separate pencil, but your drawings may not be as precise.) Make sure it can be tightened so you can use it to measure more than one circle with the same radius.

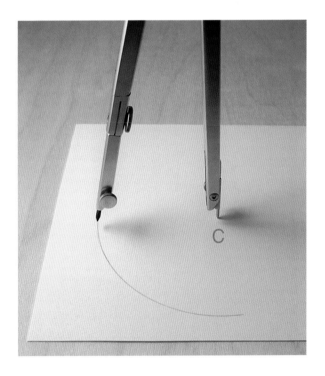

Geometry

Most of us study geometry but never get a chance to put it into practical use. In the projects section of this book you can learn how easy it is to use basic geometry to create your own symmetrically accurate constructions. Yes, you can learn to draw a perfect circle, triangle, square, pentagon or hexagon using only a compass, a pencil and a ruler. Armed with a basic understanding of simple geometry, you can create something ingenious of your own. You may never be bored by geometry again!

HORIZONTAL AXIS WIND TURBINES

Pinwheels

The first pinwheel may have been devised to frighten birds away from gardens. The continuous motion was supposed to keep birds from raiding cherry trees and strawberry patches. Probably this worked as long as the wind was blowing. However, blackbirds and jays, the most likely thieves, are also the smartest birds. They would soon realize that a moving pinwheel wasn't dangerous.

Yet the pinwheel, with its bright whirling colors, has long been a favorite toy for children of all ages. Young children will naturally run for long periods of time to keep them spinning or hold them into the wind in awe.

Pinwheels are easy to make from a variety of materials and in very little time. Parent or teacher assistance may be required to help very young children make any of the following pinwheels.

Ages 10 and up should be able to follow the simple instructions and master the basic geometry required on their own.

CONSTRUCTION TIPS

Most of the pinwheels and windmills in this book can be mounted on a wooden handle or support. To keep a windmill or pinwheel from wobbling on its axis and hitting the support, you can glue a small block of wood to the back of the fan. Make the hole through the center slightly larger than the diameter of the pin or wire that serves as your axle. Added beads help reduce friction.

A ballpoint pen body can work well as a shaft, if needed (see page 59). You may also need a rubber washer, bead or nut of some kind to cap the other end of the axle and keep it from falling out.

Some of the projects in this book may require specially purchased materials, but it pays to be a scavenger. You may be surprised how many potentially useful bits and pieces there are in your junk drawer, toy chest, toolbox or garage. Study the projects here to get ideas for ways to use materials you already have. Be resourceful in finding ways to build and hold together your creations. You will be working in the tradition of all the great inventors.

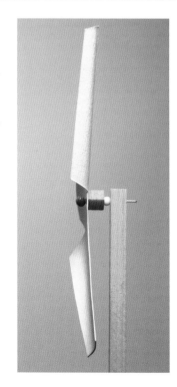

〉 2-Blade Pinwheel

What You Need
› paper, pencil, compass, ruler, scissors, pushpin, wire (about 6 in./15 cm or longer), small bead, glue (optional)

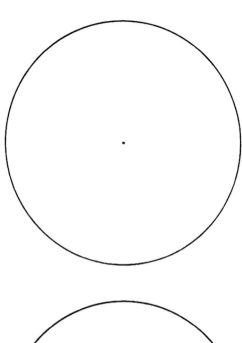

1 Draw a circle about 6 in. (15 cm) in diameter using a compass with a sharp steel point and a sharp lead.

> **Tip:** To find out the *diameter* of any circle, measure the length of a straight line through the center of the circle.

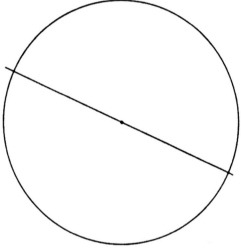

2 Draw a straight line through the center of the circle with a sharp pencil.

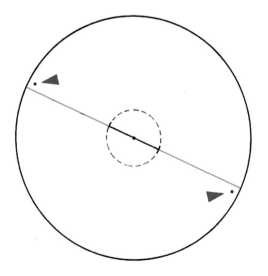

3 Draw a smaller circle around the same center point. Cut the lines shown in blue. Using a pushpin, puncture holes at the red arrows.

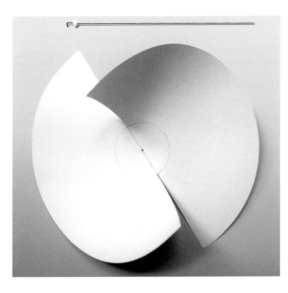

4 Curl the punctured ends so they bend in toward the center.

Make an axle from a wire bent at the end and a small glass or plastic bead. The bead is placed behind the rotor to prevent it from rubbing on the wire.

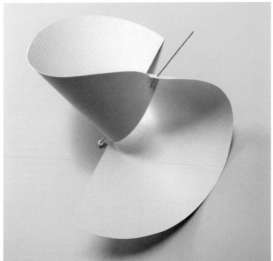

5 Push the axle through the holes as shown.

Option: You can glue the paper where the corners overlap to add stability.

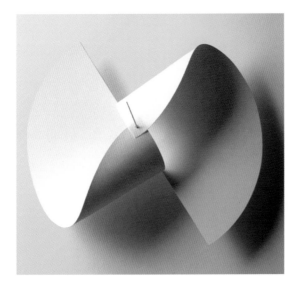

6 Hold the end of the wire axle and pull your windmill slowly through the air. Does it spin easily?

› 3-Blade Pinwheel

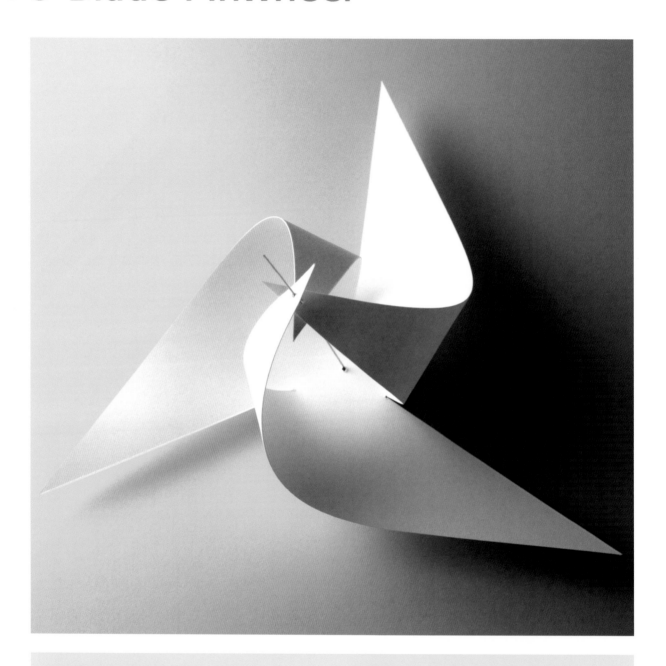

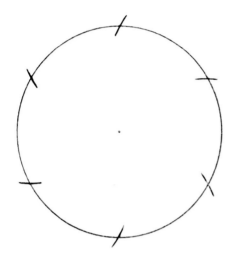 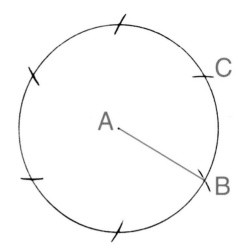

1 Using your compass, draw a circle. Depending on the size you want to make your pinwheel, the radius – the distance from the center (A) to the outside (B) of the circle – could be any measure from 3 in. (8 cm) to 10 in. (25 cm) or longer.

Without changing the size of the radius AB, move the steel point of the compass to any place on the circumference (the outside of the circle) B and draw a mark C where it intersects the circle.

Next place the steel point on C and, keeping the compass measuring the same distance, continue to mark around the circumference until it is divided into 6 equal segments.

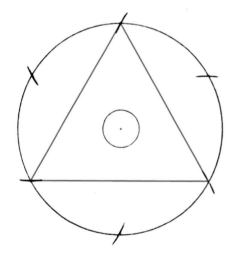 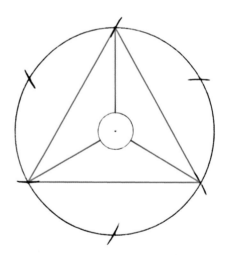

2 Cut the lines as shown in blue to create a perfect equilateral triangle. This is the shape you will be using for your pinwheel.

Draw a smaller circle inside the triangle around the same center point as you used for your original circle.

Cut as indicated in blue on a line from each tip of the triangle to the outside of the center circle. You will make 3 cuts.

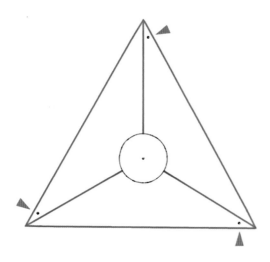

3 Puncture with a pushpin where indicated in red.

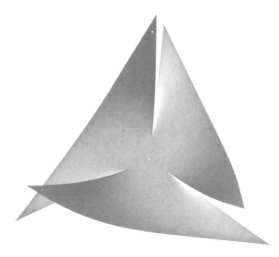

4 Curl the punctured ends in toward the center.

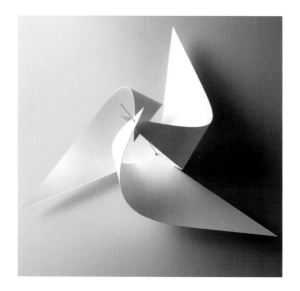

5 Thread a wire that is bent at the end and has a bead on it to reduce friction through the center base and the hole in each punctured tip. (The wire axle must be long enough to go through these 4 holes and also be held as a handle.) Glue the overlapping tips if you wish.

Test your pinwheel in various wind speeds.
Is it faster or slower than a 2-blade pinwheel?

This sturdy pinwheel is made from cereal box cardboard. It has been spray-painted blue on the printed side and mounted on a thin steel rod that fits in a hole drilled through a wooden handle. A short section of plastic tube behind the pinwheel keeps the back of rotor from touching the wood handle as it turns. (For directions on making a handle like this one, turn to page 59.)

4-Blade Pinwheel

What You Need
› paper, pencil, compass, ruler, scissors, pushpin, wire (about 6 in./15 cm or longer), small bead, glue (optional)

1 Draw a straight line (as shown in green). You will be using this straight line to help you draw a square, but not in the usual way!

Place the steel point of the compass near the mid-point of the line and draw arcs that intersect the line on either side of the center. Draw another arc directly above and another directly below the center.

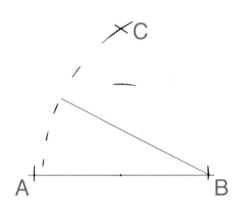

2 Place the steel point of your compass on B. Using a radius (red line) that will extend anywhere above the top arc, draw another arc as shown. Repeat this step using the same radius with the steel point of the compass on A. The arcs will intersect at C.

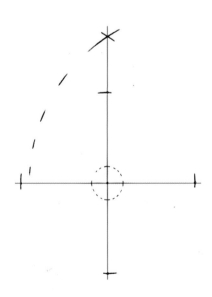

3 Draw a straight line (shown in green) from the intersecting arcs at C down through the midpoint, which is the center of the horizontal line. The green lines are perpendicular to each other (90 degrees, or square).

Draw another smaller circle around the center point.

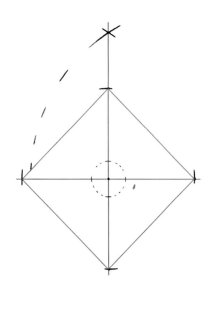

4 Join the points of intersection as shown. The red lines create a perfect square.

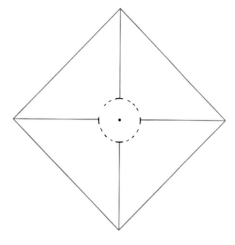

5 Cut the lines shown in blue as indicated.

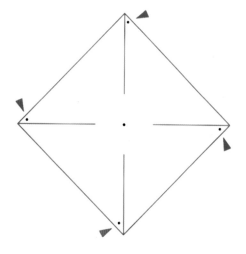

6 Using a pushpin, puncture 4 holes, one at each corner as shown.

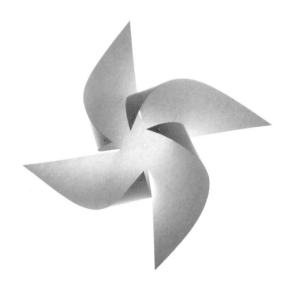

7 Curl the punctured tips in toward the center and thread a long pin or wire with a bead at the end through the holes.

8 This is a traditional pinwheel.

› 5-Blade Pinwheel

What You Need
› paper, pencil, compass, ruler, scissors, pushpin, wire (about 6 in./15 cm or longer), small bead, glue (optional)

Note: The shape you will eventually create for this pinwheel is a pentagon: 5 sides, 5 blades. This requires more advanced geometry. Study the drawings to follow along, as it gets complicated! If you have difficulty, ask for help.

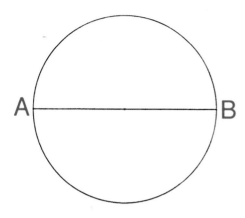

1 Using a compass, draw a circle and then draw a straight line across the circle that passes through the center point.

As long as the line passes through the center, it is the diameter of the circle.

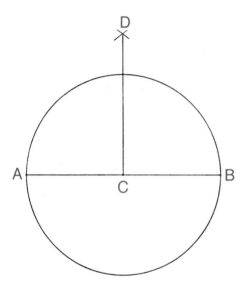

2 D will be a point you create using a radius larger than AC or AB. With the steel point of the compass placed at A and then at B, draw intersecting arcs outside the circle at D. A straight line drawn from D through the center C will give you a line perpendicular to AB.

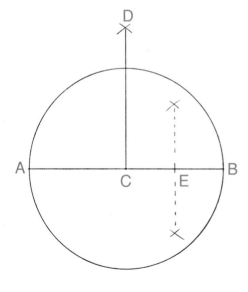

3 To divide the radius line CB in half, use C as an arc center and B as an arc center to draw intersecting arcs below and above the line. A line drawn between the intersecting arcs will divide the line CB exactly in half. The point on this line where it crosses CB is E.

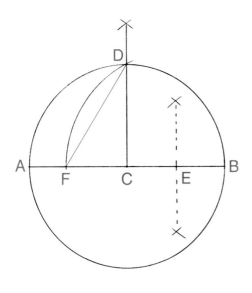

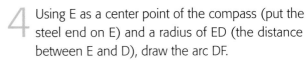
4 Using E as a center point of the compass (put the steel end on E) and a radius of ED (the distance between E and D), draw the arc DF.

The straight line FD (known as the chord) is the magic length you will use to set the new radius on the compass. Everything you have done so far has been to find out this measure.

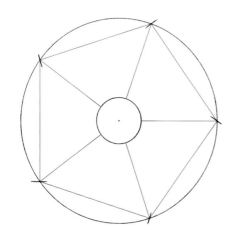

5 Using the new radius you found in step 4, place the steel point of your compass at any location on the circumference of the circle and mark where it intersects another spot on the circle. Move the steel point to the new location and continue from there around the circle marking the circumference until you have 5 marks in all.

Connect the marks on the circle to create a perfect pentagon.

Draw a smaller circle around the center point. From each point of the pentagon draw a line toward the center until it touches the small circle.

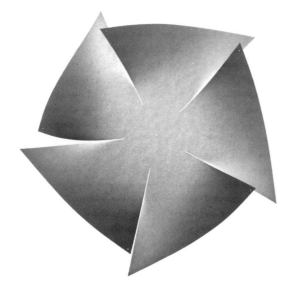

6 Cut the blue lines as indicated. If you have already built one of the simpler pinwheels, you should be able to figure out where to puncture each blade.

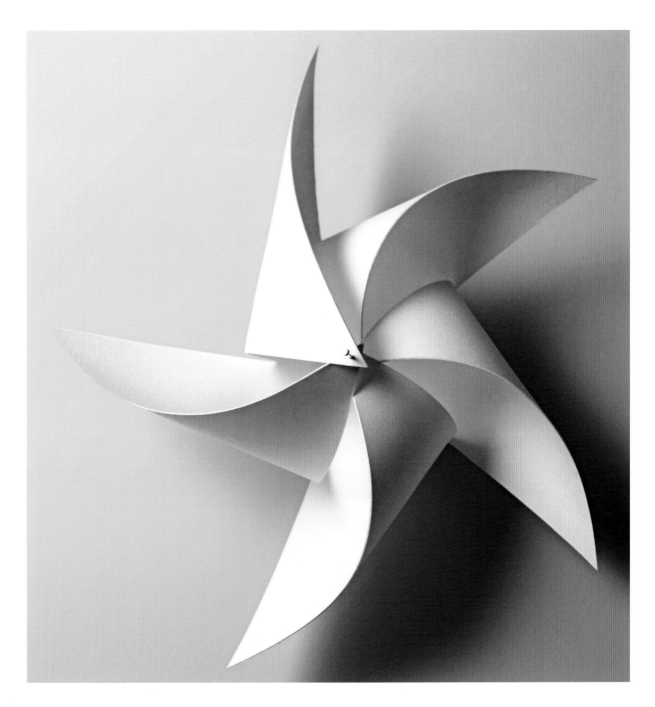

7 Curl the punctured tips in toward the center and thread a beaded pin through the holes.
When testing this pinwheel, point the front face upward to see if it will work as a vertical axis windmill.
Is there much difference between the way this pinwheel works and the way other pinwheels work?

› 6-Blade Pinwheel

What You Need
› paper, pencil, compass, ruler, scissors, pushpin, wire (about 6 in./15 cm or longer), small bead, glue (optional)

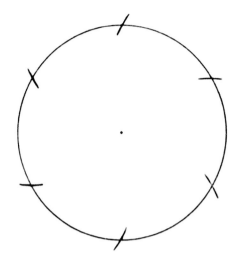

1 Draw a circle. Using the same radius, and the method described for the 3-blade pinwheel, divide the circumference into 6 equal segments.

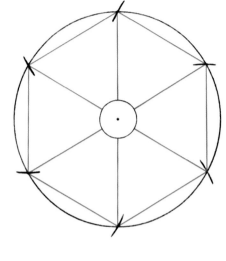

2 Connect the 6 points to create a perfect hexagon.

Draw a smaller circle around the center point. From each point of the hexagon draw a line toward the center until it touches the small circle. Cut on the lines shown in blue as indicated.

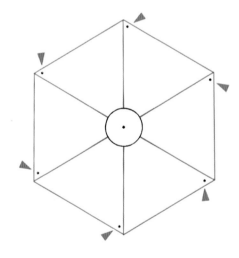

3 The red arrows show where to puncture 6 holes.

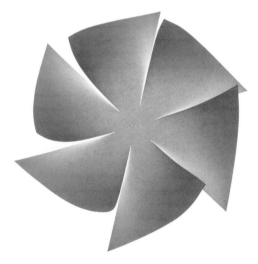

4 Curl the punctured tips in toward the center and thread a bent-ended and beaded pin through the holes. Notice this is more difficult as the number of blades increase.

Assemble as in photo at left with a wire and bead.

Experimental Windmills

Build one of the three experimental windmills in this section to get a better understanding of the problems engineers face when they design a large-scale wind turbine. By changing the length and pitch of the blades, you will be able to control the speed and power, especially in high-velocity conditions. Learn more about variable-pitch blades at page 29.

Note that the materials you use for this project (and any of the projects in this book) do not have to meet the exact same specifications described here as long as they work for you.

› X Windmill A

What You Need
› wood 3/4 in. (19 mm) thick and about 6 in. x 6 in. (15 cm x 15 cm) square
› compass
› pencil
› band saw or jig saw
› drill press
› drill press clamp
› thin steel rod (1/8 in. or 2 mm)
› Japanese saw (a handsaw good for fine cutting)
› water-based wood glue
› card stock
› wooden dowels (3/16 in. or 5 mm)
› ballpoint pen body (for X Windmill B)

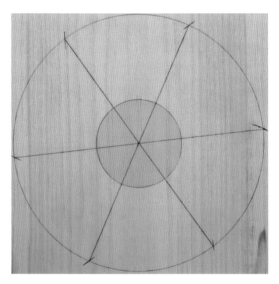

1 On a 3/4 in. (1.9 cm) thick piece of wood, draw a large circle and divide it into 6 equal segments using a compass.

Tip: See 6-Blade Pinwheel for how to divide a circle into segments.

Draw another circle the size of the hub you wish to make, like the highlighted circle in this picture.

(Having a smaller circle inside and concentric with a larger one makes dividing the smaller circle easier and more accurate when drawing the drill guide lines, especially on an irregular wood surface. Also, a larger piece of wood is easier and safer to clamp when cutting.)

2 You may need shop assistance for this task.

Cut out the hub using a band saw or jig saw.

File the outside smooth.

Lock the hub in a drill press clamp and, using the lines as guides, drill 6 3/16-in. (or 5 mm) holes around the edge. These will hold the pegs.

Drill the center hole through the hub to fit a thin steel rod. The rod will be the axle, or main shaft.

3 Cut 6 fan blade pegs (any length but at least 1 in. / 3 cm long) from the dowels and, using a fine Japanese saw, cut a slot in one end of each peg.

Find some card stock that will fit tightly into the slot. This will make it easier to remove and fit different shapes and sizes of blades.

One half of the split section can be cut away for easier gluing (see center peg) if you want to attach the fan blades permanently.

4 Cut the card stock into blades. Insert the blades and set each at the same angle in the hub.

Mount the fan on a thin steel rod with a washer or plastic bead on the back to reduce friction. Apply a strip of tape around the axle to keep the washer from slipping.

Test your variable-pitch windmill in a strong wind. Turn the blades to increase the angle to the wind so less of the face of the blade is facing the wind and observe what happens.

Change the shape and size of the blades. Here are some suggestions for blade shapes.

Use longer pegs and see what the results are.

Try making a hexagonal hub using the geometry you have learned.

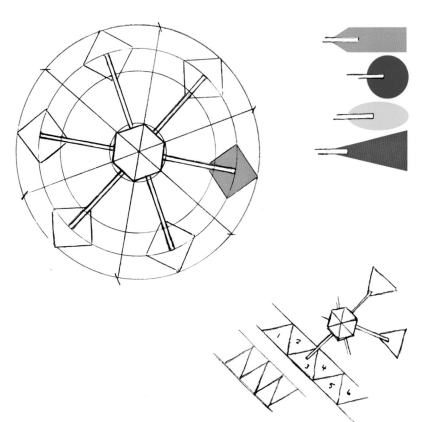

X Windmill B

This experimental fan has a square hub that was easy to cut out and drill.

The hub has a 3/16-in. (or 5 mm) center hole to fit the 3/16-in. (5 mm) axle hardwood dowel. A ballpoint pen body casing fits around the axle and is loose enough to allow it to rotate in the wind. A juice lid was used as a washer.

The square hub on this windmill makes it easy to build. Notice that one of the blades is colored to make the revolutions easier to count.

EASY TO DRILL SQUARE ROTOR HUB

JUICE LID WASHER

BALL POINT PEN BODY SECTION

VERTICAL SUPPORT

TIGHTER FITTING PEN SECTION

3 /16" DOWEL

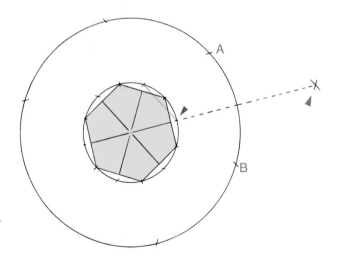

X Windmill C

Compared to the circular 6-blade hub (X Windmill A), this 6-blade hexagonal hub is easier to cut out of wood, and it is easier to drill into the flat sides.

Using the radius from the larger circle AB, draw intersecting arcs at the red arrow. You only have to find one midpoint (the green arrow) between the other marks to establish drill points.

Using the radius of the smaller circle (the red line), you can mark the other midpoints around the smaller circle.

6-Blade Windmill

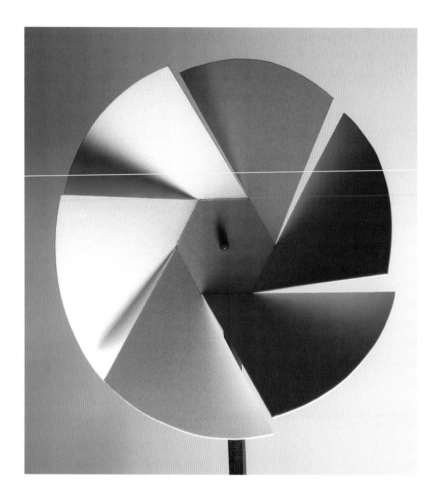

What You Need
› pencil
› paper
› compass
› ruler
› scissors
› pushpin
› wire (about 6 in./
   15 cm or longer)
› small bead

This windmill and the next one are designed like American wind pumps, which are still used to pump water for livestock.

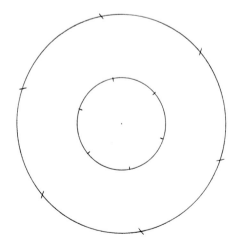

1 Draw a circle. Extend the compass so the radius is longer (here it is about twice the length) and draw another circle around the first.

Without changing the compass (keep the radius the same), divide the circumference into 6 as described for the 3- and 6-blade pinwheels. (See pages 43 and 55.)

Using a ruler placed along a line from the center to each mark on the larger circle, mark points on the smaller circle as indicated. You will have 6 marks on the outer circle and 6 marks on the inner circle.

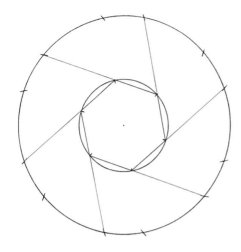

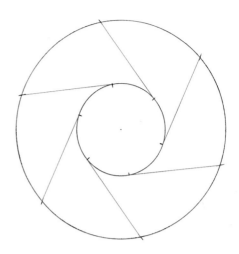

2 Draw a small hexagon by joining the 6 marks on the smaller circle (purple lines). Extend these lines out to the larger circle (blue lines).

3 Cut the lines shown in blue.

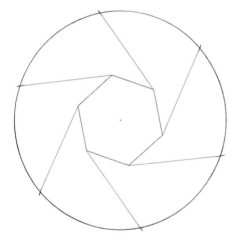

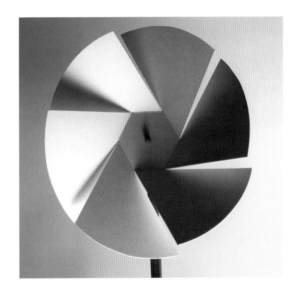

4 Score the lines shown in purple using a smooth dull tip such as a fine point ballpoint pen that has run out of ink or a small common nail. Make sure the rounded point is smooth so it won't rip the paper as you score it.

Fold the blades slightly upward from the score lines.

5 Use a long pin or stiff wire with a bead on it and bent at the end as an axle. If you wish, add another bead or two to hold it in place and reduce friction, and mount it on a long handle or support. (You can also glue a small block of wood to the back of the windmill to keep it from wobbling.)

Test this windmill in light winds.

12-Blade Windmill

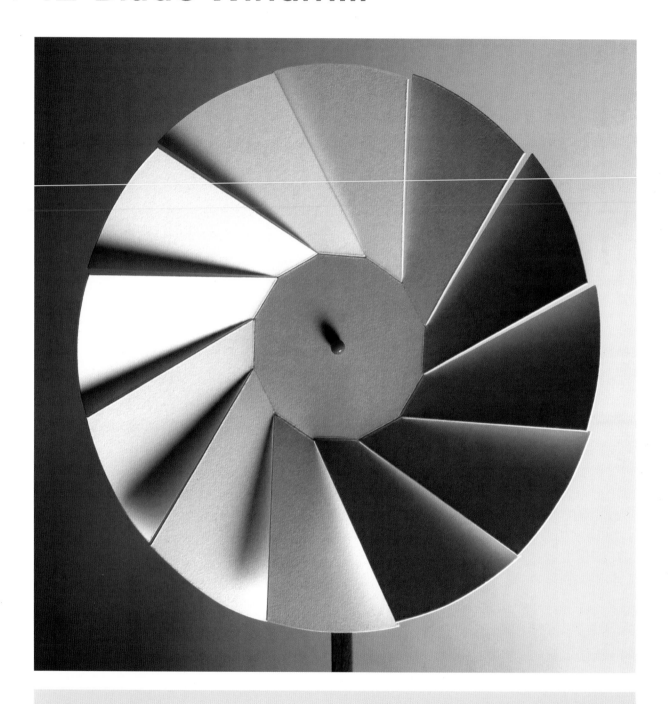

What You Need
> paper, pencil, compass, ruler, scissors, pushpin, wire (about 6 in./15 cm or longer), small bead

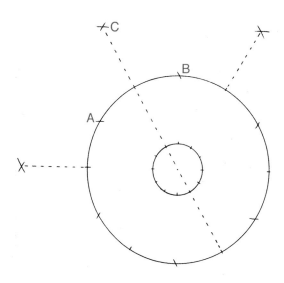

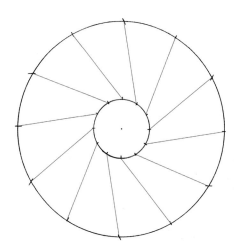

1 Start with step 1 from the 6-blade windmill. To divide the 2 circles into 12 equal arc segments you must find the midpoint between each of the 6 points. To do this, use the same radius on the compass to draw intersecting arcs outside the larger circle. Using A and B as centers, draw intersecting arcs at C.

You have to do this only 3 times, because the lines drawn into and through the center will divide the circle arc in half on the opposite side.

Mark all 12 points on both circles

2 Draw lines from each point on the small circle to the points indicated. **Note:** Look closely at the drawing. The lines do not pass through the center of the circle. The points for the lines on the larger circle are all shifted over by 1.

Cut these lines.

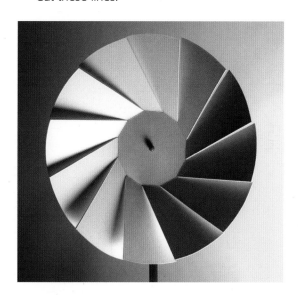

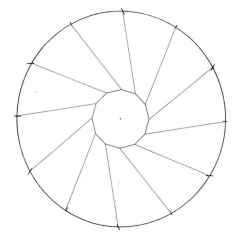

3 Score the lines shown in purple and bend the blades outward slightly.

4 Use a long pin or stiff wire with a bead on it and bent at the end as an axle. You can mount it on a wooden handle or support if you wish.

Stiff 120 lb. hot press watercolor paper was used to make this windmill so that it would hold its shape in the wind without bending backward. Test yours in different winds to see how well it holds up.

Square HAWT 1

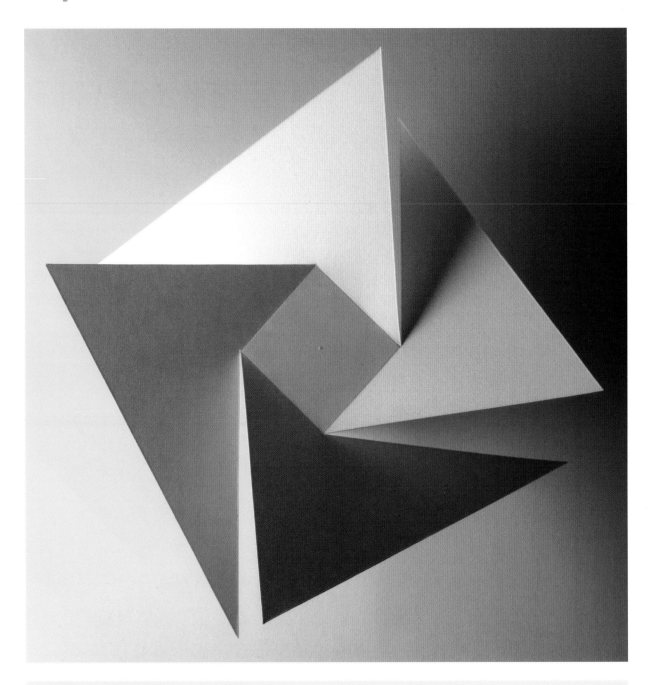

What You Need
> paper, pencil, compass, ruler, scissors, pushpin, wire (about 6 in./15 cm or longer), small bead

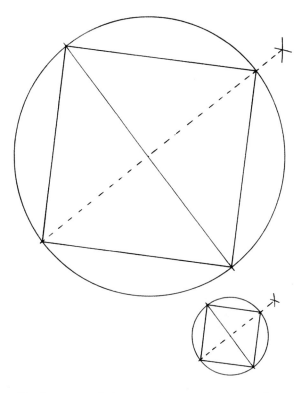

1 Draw two circles, one larger and one smaller. Draw a straight line through the center of each circle. Draw a perpendicular line through each circle center. Draw the squares in each circle at the points where the straight lines meet the circumference.

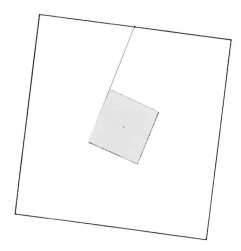

2 Cut out the smaller square. Using a pin or compass point, line up the center of the smaller square on the center of the larger square.

Rotate the smaller square until one of the sides lines up with the midpoint of one of the sides of the square. With a sharp pencil trace the outline of the smaller square.

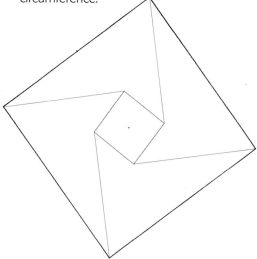

3 Draw these lines as shown. Cut the lines shown in blue and score the purple lines.

Fold each blade outward slightly.

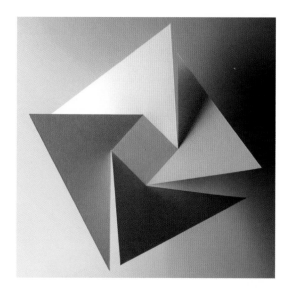

4 This propeller-like HAWT can be pulled through the air using a long wire bent and with a bead on the end.

Square HAWT 2

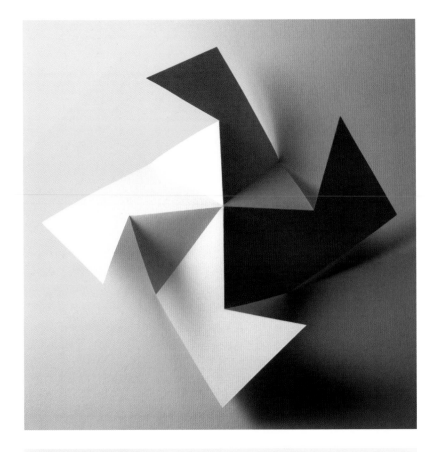

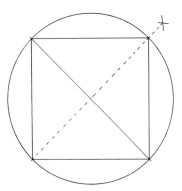

1 Draw a circle. Draw a straight line through the center of the circle. Draw a line perpendicular to the diameter. Join the 4 points to make a perfect square.

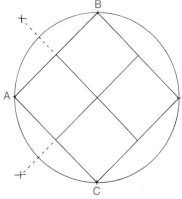

2 Using A and B as compass points (where you place the steel point of your compass), draw intersecting arcs outside the circle. Note: Any radius greater than half of the radius AB will work. Do the same thing for A and C.

Use the new points of intersection and a ruler to draw the lines through the center of the square as shown.

What You Need
› paper, pencil, compass, ruler, scissors, pushpin, wire (about 6 in./15 cm or longer), small bead

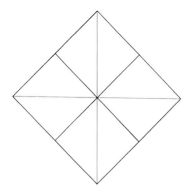

3 Divide the square from corner to corner (green lines).

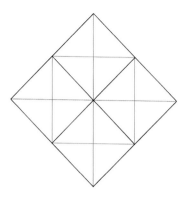

4 Draw the interior square by connecting the points as shown in red.

5 Cut the lines shown in blue. (These are the only cuts you will make.)

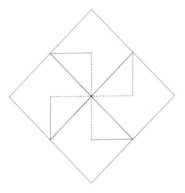

6 Score the solid purple lines on the front face. Score the dotted lines on the back face.

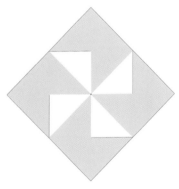

7 The 4 light blue shapes are flat blades. The white triangles connect them.

8 Carefully fold the scores to make this odd propeller-shaped HAWT.

Push a long beaded wire through the center and test it to see if it spins effectively when pulled through the air.

6-Blade Star

What You Need
› paper, pencil, compass, ruler, scissors, pushpin, wire (about 6 in./15 cm or longer), small bead

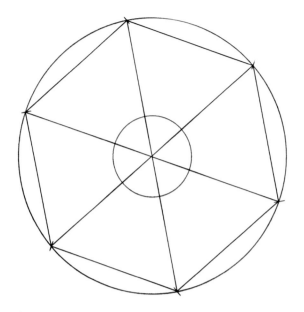

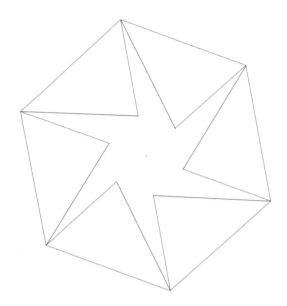

1 Draw a small circle then a larger one around it. Draw a straight line through the center of the circles. Using the radius of the larger circle, mark the 6 points on the circumference as in the 3- and 6-blade pinwheels. Connect the points to draw a hexagon.

2 See if you can figure out where to cut and where to score using this drawing as a guide. Note the circular symmetry.

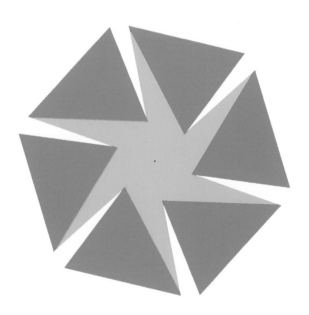

3 The darker triangles are the blades. The lighter star is the flat hub.

4 Variations of this star can be made by changing the size of the small circle. See if you can make one with larger blades and a smaller hub.

Push a long beaded wire through the center to use as an axle. How well does your star turn in the wind?

›X HAWT A

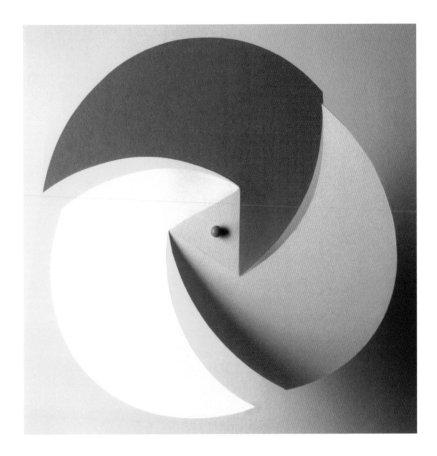

EXPERIMENTAL HAWTS

The three experimental HAWTs on this page, the Sunflower Turbine and Modern Turbines, and the experimental windmills at pages 66–59 are all good starting places for your own HAWT designs. Remember the pros and cons of HAWTS versus VAWTs (see pages 32–33) when planning your creation.

What You Need
› pencil
› paper
› compass
› ruler
› scissors
› pushpin
› wire (about 6 in./ 15 cm or longer)
› small bead

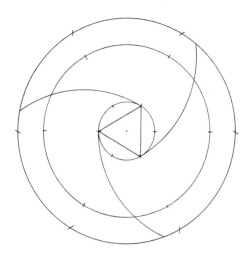

1 Don't let this drawing confuse you. The triangle is the hub and that is where the blades are scored. A smaller hub creates less resistance to the wind and larger blades generate more power.

Figure out where the center points are for the arcs. Using what you have learned so far about using a compass and working with circular symmetry, draw your own set of circles.

Divide the circles into 6, using a compass to mark them as when drawing a hexagon. (See 3- and 6-blade pinwheels.)

Look at the photo and determine where the score lines have to be and where to cut.

2 This design for a small compact turbine works efficiently in light wind but could only be used on a small scale to generate a small amount of electricity. If this were built with a diameter of 10 feet it would rip itself apart in high winds or blow the tower over.

Any design must suit the application for which it is intended. A design such as this might be perfect to generate enough electricity to charge a battery for a cell phone or a radio.

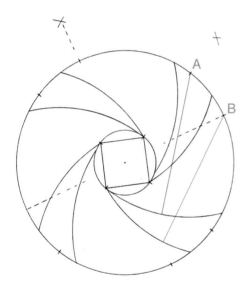

X HAWT B

This is a drawing for a 4-bladed turbine that has gaps between the blades to allow passing wind to escape more effectively.

A and B are centers for the arcs they touch. Once you have established where you wish to place an arc, you have to find the other 3 center points around the circle.

Study the drawing to see how this was done.

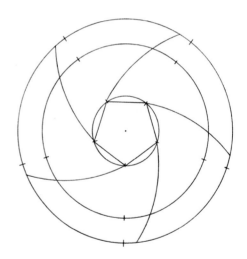

X HAWT C

You learned how to divide a circle into 5 to make a pentagon when creating a 5-blade pinwheel. Now figure out how to draw the 5 arcs that separate the blades.

› Sunflower Turbine

What You Need
› pencil
› compass
› 120 lb. hot press watercolor paper
› scissors
› small block of wood
› drill
› glue
› ballpoint pen body
› cap nut
› wood for handle

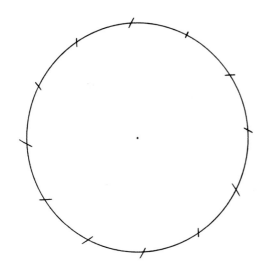

1 Draw a 6–8-in. (150–200 mm) circle on a piece of 120 lb. hot press watercolor paper. This will become the rotor of your turbine.

Using a compass, divide the circle into 12 or 16 equal segments. Choose a big enough piece of paper. You will be tracing blades around the outside of your circle, so your paper should be large enough to include those. Do not cut your circle yet.

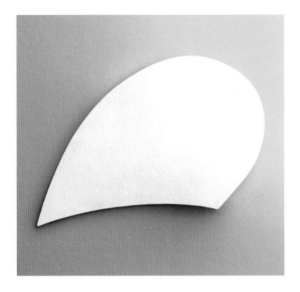

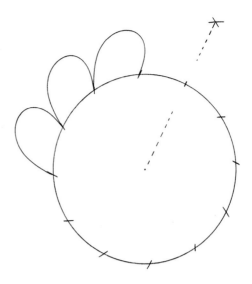

2 Take a separate piece of paper and draw an arc (at least as long as one segment of the circle) with the same radius as your circle.

Cut along the arc, leaving enough paper outside the circle to draw a single blade for a pattern for tracing.

Place the arc on your circle and mark the arc length of any segment on the circumference. Draw your blade shape from these points. Cut out your blade pattern and trace it to draw blades around your circle (which you have already drawn but not yet cut).

Cut out the rotor. The complete rotor (circle and blades) will end up looking like the blade of a circular saw. (See the next photo.)

3 After curling all the blades carefully (see photo), cut a hole in the center of the rotor for the axle to pass through.

Using a drill press for precision, drill a small block of wood with a hole the size of the axle. Glue the block to the back side of the rotor as shown, exactly at the center.

Glue and insert the axle in the block, leaving it longer than you might need. This photo shows the inside block of wood and the axle glue in place.

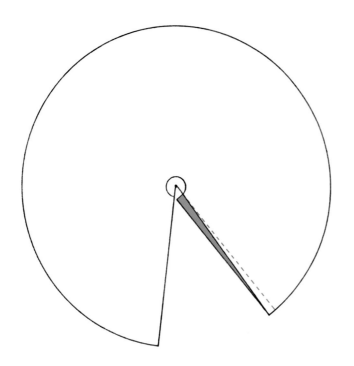

4 To make a cone, cut out a section of the circle as indicated, using radial lines. Your pattern should include the green triangle; otherwise, you won't be able to glue the tiny overlap close to the center. The red dotted line is the overlap limit.

Make a test cone from an inexpensive piece of paper first to make sure the overlap will work and the cone is the shape you want. Note that the small hole at the center of the cone should be slightly bigger than the tube that contains the axle.

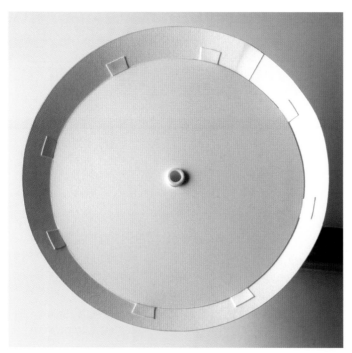

5 To make a cap to enclose and stiffen the cone, cut out a circle slightly smaller than the cone circle. Create tabs for gluing by snipping symmetrically around the circumference of the circle. Score the tabs so they will bend smoothly around the edge of the circle.

Insert the ballpoint pen body tube through the cone and the back circle.

With the pointed side of the cone pointing down into a perfectly round receptacle (an empty yogurt container will do), center the backing circle and glue the tabs to the inside of the cone.

6 Although this looks as if it might be the front of your sunflower turbine, it is the back. The other side will face into the wind.

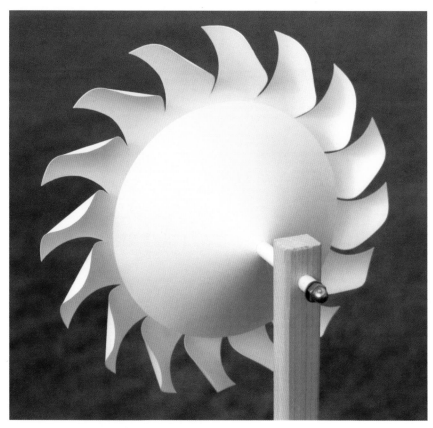

7 Assemble the pieces as shown in the photographs. Insert the pen body into a hole drilled into a support piece of wood used for a handle.

Cut off the extra length of axle and screw on a cap nut to prevent the axle from coming out of the tube. Adjust the cone so it doesn't rub on the rotor when it turns. If necessary, apply tape on the inside to prevent it from slipping.

Face the cone apex into the wind and watch it fly. Try different blade shapes.

Modern Wind Turbines

Modern wind turbines are designed to withstand extremes in wind conditions. They have to be able to turn in light winds and yet also operate and not fly apart in a gale. The space between the blades allows the fouled air to pass before the next blade passes through the same zone.

As used here, fouled air doesn't mean noxious or smelly. When the flow of air has been disturbed, it is fouled. So the space between the blades allows the air that has already been moved to escape before the next blade comes along. For more on fouling, see Some Basic Principles at page 22.

Whether these turbines are 10 feet or 200 feet in diameter, they are engineered for maximum power and strength. The aerodynamic shape of the blades allows the faster-moving tips to pass through the air with minimum turbulence. The wider sections closer to the hub have a greater pitch (they are angled more) to produce greater power.

› Modern Turbine

What You Need
› 3/4 in. (19 mm) dowel, 3/16 in. (5 mm) dowel, 120 lb. hot press watercolor paper, glue, 3 in. (80 mm) length of plastic tubing (or a ballpoint pen body), drill, length of wood for support

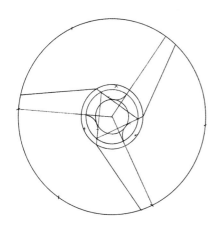

1 This is a drawing for a paper version of a modern wind turbine. Circles have been used in the drawing to help you determine points that are symmetrical with each other. Try drawing your own version of this to see if you can master the symmetry. Look at the next drawing and photo of this project so you understand what you are trying to do.

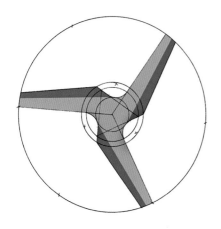

2 The lighter blue is the part that is flat to the wind, that is, the part that will face the wind. The darker blue is curled forward to create the pitch. You can use a rounded blunt tool to score between the darker and lighter blue areas to help curl the darker section forward.

3 This is the shape you are trying to create. Note that a section of round dowel will be glued to the center of the back. It has a hole drilled in it to accommodate an axle. See the construction photo, next.

4 The axle passes loosely through a section taken from a ballpoint pen body. The handle or support has been drilled to hold the pen body snugly. A tight-fitting washer prevents the axle from moving backward. These easy-to-find parts take the place of the steel bearings and shafts found in larger working turbines.

5 This photo shows this turbine in a strong wind. Note how blurred the tips of the blades are compared to the part of the blades that is closer to the hub. This is visual proof that the tips of the blades are moving faster.

Modern Turbine with Airfoil Blades

Making airfoil-shaped blades from paper is not as difficult as you might think. However, it is next to impossible to make blades with compound curves like the ones used on huge modern turbines. See the photograph on page 27 for an example of the real thing.

What You Need
› pencil
› 90 lb. hot press watercolor paper
› scissors
› ruler
› small block or wheel of wood for hub
› 3/16 in. (5 mm) wooden dowels
› drill
› glue
› ballpoint pen body
› washer
› cap nut
› length of wood for support

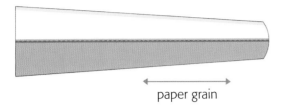

paper grain

The best paper to use to construct an airfoil blade is 90 lb. hot press watercolor paper because it is stiff enough to hold its shape and strong enough to stand up in a strong wind. Before you draw your pattern, test the paper to determine the direction of the grain. Do this by curling the paper over a wooden dowel and seeing if it makes a smooth curve without cracking. Score lightly along the center line (purple) to help bend the 2 halves together over the dowel.

The center line curve over the dowel will be the leading edge of the foil. The trailing edge where the two edges meet is glued (light yellow) flat and is the trailing edge of the foil.

Once you have carefully managed to get the two edges of the trailing edge to meet, apply glue sparingly along the edges with a stiff piece of paper and press them together, holding them down with the edge of a ruler.

Trailing edge

Leading edge

2. Once your blade is dry, you can insert a 3/16-in. (5 mm) dowel with a small amount of glue on one side and stick it to the inside of the leading edge.

After the glue has dried you can curve the middle of the blade slightly to finish the airfoil shape. Using the same pattern, make 2 more blades.

3. Use your block or wheel of wood to create a round hub with 3 equally spaced holes or, if you have your 6-blade hub from the X Windmill A project at page 56, you can use every second hole for this turbine. Using a short length of dowel, the ballpoint pen body, washer and nut, mount the hub on the wood support.

Note how efficiently it moves in a strong breeze.

› VERTICAL AXIS WIND TURBINES

› 2-Blade VAWT

What You Need
› paper, pencil, compass, ruler, scissors, glue, stiff wire or rod for axis, length of wood for support, split-shot fishing sinkers

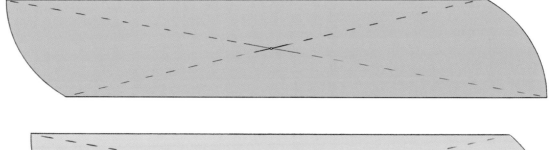

1 Draw a parallelogram and add a curve to each of the shorter ends as shown. Find the center point by drawing diagonals from the corners. Make a second parallelogram by tracing the first. These are the horizontal blade supports.

Cut out 2 rectangles of paper for the blades (the length is up to you) and curl them to fit the curves on the ends of the supports. Mark the inside of the blades so you know where to glue. The blades can be the same width as the supports or wider as long as they are both the same.

Using a small strip of paper, apply glue to the curved ends of the blade supports then hold the blade in place for 30 seconds until it will not separate. Allow 2 minutes for drying before you glue the other end.

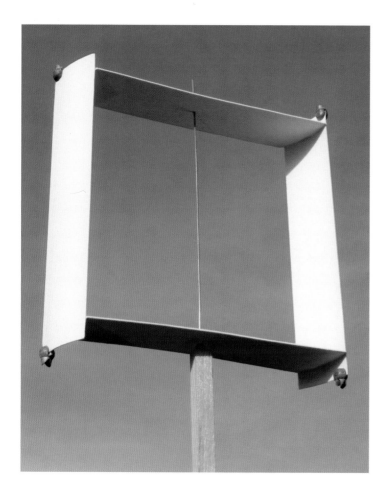

2 Use an awl or drill to make a small hole to fit the axle snugly in the wooden support. Feed the axle through the center of the blade supports.

Try blowing on the turbine to see if it will revolve. Hold it in a breeze to see if it will start to move. If it stays in one position, start it to see if it will continue to spin. If it stops, add split-shot fishing sinkers to the ends as shown. This will give additional centrifugal force and momentum to the turbine to keep it moving.

Note the pulse — the rhythmic beat — as the turbine spins. As the rotor turns it goes in and out of phase with the wind, causing a noticeable pulse. This pulse is one of the inherent problems with this type of turbine.

VENTILATOR

This prototype ventilator-style VAWT was exposed to too much humidity, and the blades curled and twisted because the paper used was a little too thin. When it was first made it performed about as well as any rooftop ventilator. You may not want to try to duplicate this design, but it could be the inspiration for something else.

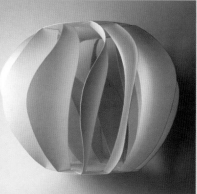

This kind of turbine may not be ideal for generating large amounts of electricity but may have a future for continuous use to silently charge automobile batteries or for household backup in case of power failures.

It's interesting to note that all the blades warped in exactly the same way. Because all the blades were affected similarly, the symmetry was not affected and the unit still performed much as it did before.

3-Blade VAWT

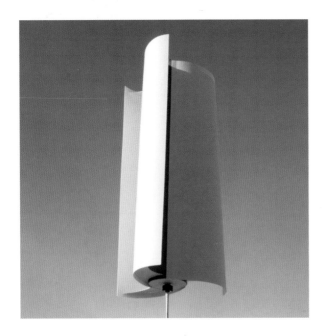

What You Need
› pencil, cardboard from paper towel roll, paper, compass, ruler, French curve, scissors, glue, stiff wire or steel rod

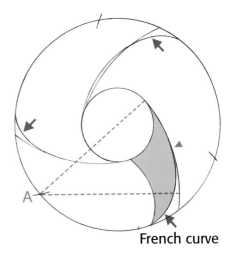

French curve

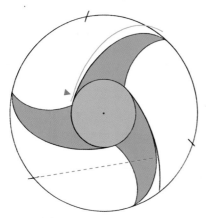

1 Take an undamaged tube from a paper towel roll (show here in light green) and measure the exact diameter. Cut out 2 circles that will fit the ends perfectly.

Before gluing the circles to the ends, using a compass, divide the circumference of the top circle into 3. Vertical lines from these marks will be the equal spacing guides for glueing the blades and blade supports (dark green).

On a separate piece of paper draw the diameter of the tube and another larger circle to represent the outside reach of the blades. Divide the larger circle into 3 and mark the points on the circumference. Using a compass, set a radius that extends from one of the points to the opposite side of the smaller circle (dotted red line), and draw an arc.

Mark the midpoint of the arc (red arrow). Using a *French curve* (a template used to draw smooth curves, commonly used in drafting and dressmaking), draw an ever-decreasing curve until it touches the outside circle. This curved line marks the location of the edge of the support that the blades will be glued to.

Draw a straight or curved line that will be the position of the trailing edge of the support (a curved trailing edge support is shown here), making sure that it will leave enough room on the tube for the blades to be glued without overlapping. Cut out 6 support struts that are all the same.

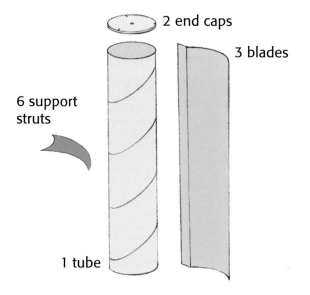

2 end caps

3 blades

6 support struts

1 tube

2   Cut out 3 blades the length of the tube with a width to fit the leading edge of the supports (see solid orange line in first drawing). Score a full-length tab along the inside edge of the blade for gluing.

Curve the blades by curling them over the edge of a table or other rounded object until they match the curvature of the leading edge of the supports.

Glue the blade tabs symmetrically around the tube.

Edge glue the supports at each end, first to the tube and then to the support and hold in place until dry.

3   The finished turbine should look something like the turbine in the photos at right.

The curvature of the leading edge can vary. You can use different tubing for the center axis. If gluing is too difficult, tape can be used to hold the pieces in place.

4   This turbine spun very fast and silently in a light breeze. The tighter curve toward the end of the blades seemed to create a better airfoil, causing less resistance on the blade as it moved into the wind on the drag side of its rotation.

〉X 3-Blade VAWT

What You Need

> pencil, cardboard, paper, ruler, scissors, glue, wooden dowels, 3/16 in. (5 mm)

stiff wire or steel rod, elastic bands (3), bearings or plastic sleeves (2)

1 Draw and cut out 2 equalilateral triangles from stiff 3-ply cardboard. Drill holes near the corners of the triangles to accommodate 3 dowels. Glue the dowels into the bottom triangle, making sure they dry in position at 90 degrees to the base.

Cut out 3 pieces of paper 1/4 in. (6 mm) shorter than the length of the dowels. Fold them over and glue the ends. Bend them to form curved airfoil shapes and slip them over the dowels as shown.

Fit the remaining triangle on top and hold it tightly together with knotted elastics through the holes as shown. If possible, find 2 bearings or plastic sleeves and fit them to the center holes of the triangles to reduce friction. Insert a straight wire axis.

2 Rotate the blades around the dowels to try different positions making sure all three are on the same angle. Test the unit to see what works best.

Change the shape and size of the blades. Try using 90-degree or 180-degree C-sections of cardboard from paper towel rolls. Test it and other different shapes to see how the shape affects the performance.

3 In this experimental VAWT the rotor spun fairly well but in a light breeze it had to be started manually.

This particular example is like the Savonius (see page 88), because the wind will catch on the convex side and be deflected on the opposite side as the rotor turns into the wind.

Easy 6-Blade VAWT

What You Need
› pencil, corrugated cardboard, paper, compass, ruler, French curve, knife, glue, stiff wire or steel rod

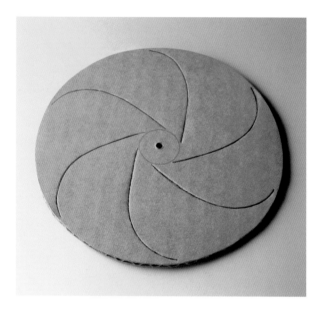

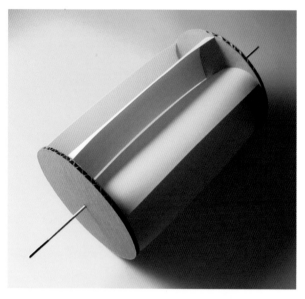

1 Draw a curve with a compass and modify it with a French curve to create a template that you think might work well for a blade shape.

Divide a circle of corrugated cardboard into 6 and trace the template symmetrically around the circle. Make another one, but a mirror of the first, remembering to flip the template so the cuts will match opposite each other. Cut through the curves without cutting into the bottom layer of cardboard.

Cut out 6 blades that are all the same length and have a width the same as the curves. Curl the blades over the edge of a table so they match the curves cut into the circles.

Insert all the blades into one of the circles. Then starting on one side of the other circle, slowly push the blades in until all of the blades are inserted. The blades will not have to be glued as the edges of the corrugated will pinch the blades preventing them from coming out.

This is easy and fast enough to build that you can try any number of different configurations.

2 The finished turbine will look something like this.

3 This turbine performed very well in a very light wind. The spinning blades appeared as a blur.

6-Blade VAWT

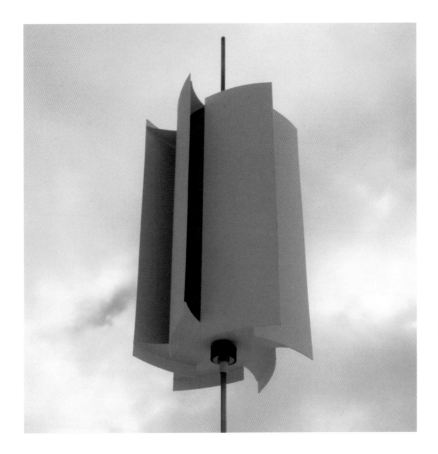

Note: This project demands step-by-step patience and care. If you have forgotten the geometry and how to draw using a compass, see the 3-Blade Pinwheel instructions to refresh your memory. If you are still puzzled, ask someone for help.

What You Need
› pencil
› paper towel roll or other cardboard tube
› heavy cardboard
› paper
› compass
› ruler
› knife
› glue
› stiff wire or steel rod
› bead or other bearing

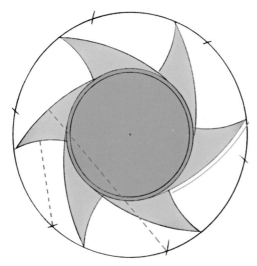

1 This VAWT is made with the end cap and blade supports all in one piece (dark blue and light blue areas). The all-in-one end caps do not have to be lined up to support the blades in a vertical position. If you decide to offset the ends slightly, all the blades will have a slight twist to them. They will all have the same twist as long as the ends are centered on the ends of the tube.

Start by measuring the diameter of an undamaged cardboard tube. Use half of that measure for the radius of your compass. Draw a circle centered on a piece of stiff paper or cardboard. Using the same center, draw a larger circle that will be the circle of rotation for the tips of the blades. You choose the size.

Divide the larger circle into 6 using the same radius to mark the circumference. Reset your compass to a radius that will reach from any of the marks to the far side of the tube circle (dotted red line) and draw an arc that extends to the large circle. Draw all 6 arcs.

Find a suitable radius that will produce an arc that connects the outside of the tube circle to the larger circle (dotted green line). Find the other 5 points around the large circle to draw the other smaller arcs.

Decide at this point if you want the blades to be vertically straight or twisted.

Cut out the 2 complete end pieces and glue them to the ends of the tube by using the drawn tube diameter circles to align the ends.

Cut out the blades using the outside of the blade supports for width measurement (orange line).

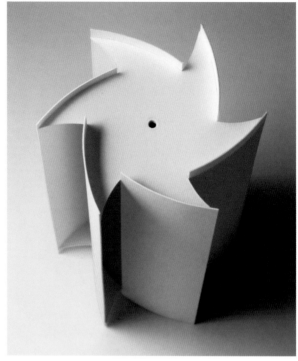

2 Keep in mind that the length of the blades can extend beyond the supports or be cut to the exact length of the tube. The photo here shows the blades extending slightly beyond the supports. This made the blades easier to glue.

Apply glue to the edge of the support and hold the blade in place against the curved edge until it holds fast enough to release pressure. Glue all blades into position.

Use the centers on the ends made by the compass to make holes big enough for your axle.

To reduce friction add bearings or plastic sleeves or wax the axle.

3 In a sudden squall the rotor seems to be spinning at very high rpm. Try applying slight pressure on the underside of the rotor and watch how quickly it slows down. This is typical of all VAWTs — they slow down very quickly when any load is applied.

Note the bearing used on the axle to reduce friction.

› Savonius

What You Need
› pencil
› heavy cardboard
› paper
› compass
› ruler
› knife
› glue
› stiff wire or steel rod
› small bead or washer
› tape
› balsa or other light wood strip (optional)

1 Draw a line and find the center point.

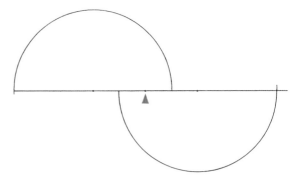

2 From the center point, mark a point on either side of the center as shown. Use each of those marks to center the compass and draw 2 half circles overlapping each other on opposite sides.

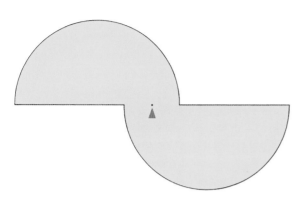

3 Cut out the shape shown in yellow from stiff 3-ply cardboard. Make another exactly the same. These 2 shapes are the top and bottom supports for the blades.

Make 2 blades that have a width equal to the half circle arcs out of stiff paper. Curl the paper to match the curvature of the half circles.

Edge glue the paper blades to the supports.

Insert a straight wire through both ends. Wrap the wire with a piece of tape and add a bead or washer to keep the rotor from sliding down.

4 The finished turbine should look something like this. Note that the edge of the paper has been reinforced with a strip of wood to keep it straight.

5 This turbine moved in the slightest breeze. This type of turbine is used for anemometers or where continuous motion will provide a small amount of electricity, for example, as may be required for an offshore light buoy.

› Squirrel Cage

What You Need
› pencil
› stiff flat paper
› compass
› metal ruler
› knife
› glue
› stiff wire or steel rod
› length of wood for support

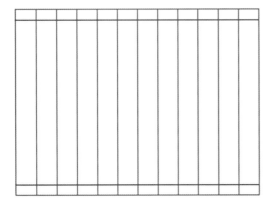

1 Using stiff flat paper, draw all the blades together in one block. Score all the blades as indicated by the purple lines then cut the blades (as shown by the blue lines). This will give you 12 blades that are all the same. By scoring the paper you created tabs at both ends of each strip: fold them over 90 degrees as shown so they are ready to glue.

2 Cut out 2 circles of 2-ply paper the same size and divide the circumferences into 12. Mark the points clearly on each.

Save the paper the circles were cut from to make a small template (bottom left). Take another small piece of paper and glue it to the surface of the first, choosing an angle you think might work. (Here the angle is offset 20 degrees.)

Now when you place this template overlapping the circles at each point you can draw a faint line for gluing the blades in place accurately.

When gluing, use a thin strip of paper to apply the glue. Press the tabs down flat with a chopstick or narrow piece of wood.

Turn the construction upside down and carefully glue each blade tab to the other circle at the 12 corresponding marks, being careful not to twist the blades.

3 The turbine can be tall and thin or short and wide. Try different angles on the blades.

4 This is what your finished turbine should look like.

5 Mount the turbine on a vertical support using a thin wire for an axis.

In this photo the turbine spins very fast. Try slowing the turbine by placing your finger on the spinning edge to see how much power it has.

THE FUTURE OF WINDPOWER

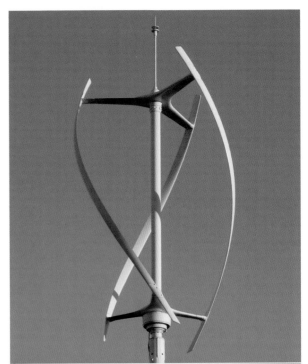

The future looks positive for wind power. Yet wind power is only part of the solution to produce energy in a sustainable way by phasing out air polluting technologies. New advancements in solar, geothermal, hydro, hydrogen fuel cell and tidal power will inevitably be part of the mix. Time is critical for implementing these new technologies as our biosphere has to absorb more and more pollutants from burning carbon-based fuels. Currently the push is on for bigger wind turbines because there is more money to be made from more and larger turbines to feed the electrical power grid. But what happens when all of us are driving electric cars and plugging them into the grid for recharging? This will put an even greater strain on the grid and create a neverending increase in demand for mega-projects.

Part of the solution is in smaller wind devices that will allow individuals to become more self sufficient. If an electric car can be recharged by a small wind turbine overnight, then that is a real contribution to solving emission problems. If we choose to recharge batteries for laptops, cordless tools, cameras and cell phones from a micro wind turbine and to operate low-power-consuming electronics, then there will be less demand put on the grid. If we are smart enough to choose the right direction to truly solve these growing problems, if we have enough time, and if and only if each of us are willing to change....

GLOSSARY

Aerodynamics The dynamics of solid bodies moving through air.

Airfoil Also aerofoil (British); a structure with curved surfaces (e.g. wing, fin or tail plane) designed to give lift in flight.

Anemometer An instrument for measuring wind force and speed.

Arc A segment of a curve.

Archimedes screw An ancient apparatus for raising water, consisting of either a spiral tube around an inclined axis or an inclined tube containing a tight-fitting, broad-threaded screw.

Axis A straight line about which a body or geometrical object rotates, as in the axle of a wheel; also, a line segment serving to orient a space or geometrical object, especially a line about which the object is symmetrical.

Betz's Law This states that it is only possible to capture 59.6 percent of the energy in the wind, which is the best compromise between blocking the wind entirely or the opposite of allowing it all to pass. Obviously, in order to keep the rotor moving continuously you have to allow some wind to pass through the circle of rotation. This is the compromise any wind device must make whether it is a farm water pump or a huge wind turbine used to generate electricity.

Camber A slightly arched surface such as the surface of an airfoil.

Centrifugal force The force on a body in curvilinear motion that is directed away from the center of curvature or axis. Like the outward force that draws the water from your clothes in a washing machine in the spin cycle.

Circle of rotation The circle within which the rotor spins. The longer the blades of a wind turbine, the greater its circle of rotation.

Concentric Having the same center.

Diameter The length of a straight line through the center of a circle.

Drag The slowing force exerted on a moving body by a fluid medium, the force on the surface of an object moving through a fluid to slow it down.

Fantail A mechanical fan shaped mechanism of a windmill that moves the main blades into the wind.

Fixed mills Windmills that face into the prevailing winds and do not rotate.

Fouled air Disturbed turbulent air left in the wake of a moving object such as a sail or windmill blade.

French curve Any curve taken from a spiral where the radius is constantly changing; also, a tool used for dressmaking and pattern-drawing.

Furl To roll and up secure (a sail) to a yard or mast.

Governor A feedback device on a machine or engine used to provide automatic speed control.

Grid Network of electricity supply lines that criss-cross the country.

Leading edge The dynamic edge that leads a wing or airfoil into a moving stream of air to separate the stream with the least resistance, as in the front edge of an airplane wing.

Lift The component of the total aerodynamic force acting on an airfoil, or aircraft, perpendicular to the relative wind and normally exerted in an upward direction, opposing the pull of gravity.

Load The resistance applied to a main shaft of a windmill by gears or pulleys to perform work or generate electricity.

Luff To flap back and forth while losing wind.

Main shaft The primary axle or drive shaft of a windmill with attached blades or sails.

Nacelle The housing unit behind the rotor of a modern wind turbine that supports the hub, gears, generator and controls.

Overspeed The speed of a tuning rotor that has gone beyond the safe recommended speed causing excessive strain on all components and eventual destruction.

Perpendicular Two lines or planes that form congruent adjacent right (90-degree) angles, as in a T.

Pitch The set angle of a blade relative to the oncoming wind.

Polder mill A windmill used to pump water.

Post mill An early type of windmill that uses a post around which the entire mill rotates allowing the sails to face into the wind.

Radius A line segment that joins the center of a circle with any point on its circumference. Also, the distance from the center point of the circle to any point on its circumference.

Reefing The use of ties on a sail to reduce sail area.

Rotor Any mechanical device that rotates in a circle when faced into the wind (includes the hub and the blades).

Score Using a dull point to indent a fold line in paper.

Self-furling sails Sails that automatically reduce sail area in a strong wind by rolling the sail around a spar.

Spar Pole or mast that sails are attached to.

Spring sails Windmill sails held tight by springs; the sails angle away from a strong gust of wind to prevent damage to the spars and sails.

Template Also known as a jig. A pattern or temporary piece used for drawing, cutting or piecing together a project, often made from less costly materials than the final project.

Tjasker An ancient windmill, usually small, used to pump water by means of an inclined Archimedes screw.

Torque The moment and tendency of a force and the measure of how much that force acting upon an object causes that object to rotate.

Tower mill An early type of windmill that has a stationary body with a rotating cap and main shaft that can be moved to allow the sails to face windward.

Trailing edge The tapered edge at the back end of a blade or wing that allows the separated air stream above and below a wing to converge.

Turbine Rotary motor driven by the flow of water, steam or wind.

Turbulence The disturbance of flow caused by any object in the path of moving water or air.

Variable-pitch blades Some windmill have these blades that can change their angle to the wind to operate more efficiently and to prevent damage in gale conditions.

SOURCES AND RESOURCES

Books

Baker, T. Lindsay. *A Field Guide to American Windmills*. University of Oklahoma Press, 1985.

Gipe, Paul. *Wind Energy Basics*. Chelsea Green, 2009. And other books by Paul Gipe.

Hills, Richard L. *Power from Wind: A History of Windmill Technology*. Cambridge University Press, 1994

Walker, Niki. *Generating Wind Power*. Crabtree Publishing Company, 2006.

Yorke, Stan. *Windmills and Waterwheels Explained*. Countryside Books, 2006.

Web

The International Molinological Society (TIMS): www.timsmills.info

Danish Wind Industry Association www.windpower.org

The Franklin Institute educational wind energy links: http://www.fi.edu/learn/hotlists/wind.php

Paul Gipe website: www.wind-works.org

NASA website: www.nasa.gov
To use their interactive airfoil simulator, go to the search box and enter: FOILSIM

For historic issues of *Scientific American* magazine: www.scientificamericanpast.com

wikipedia.org
enter windmills, wind turbines or wind power in the search box

World Meteorological Organization: www.wmo.int.

Photo Credits

All photographs by the author except as otherwise noted.

Many thanks to those individuals and organizations who contributed photographs for this book. Pages 2-3, © Ilona Budzbon; page 6, ©Terrance Emerson/ iStockphoto; page 9, © Oliver Childs/ iStockphoto; page 14 (top left) © Mlenny Photography | Alexander Hafemann/ iStockphoto, (top right) © Steffen Hoejager/Shutterstock, (bottom) © asterix0597/iStockphoto; page 15 (top) courtesy of Silver Spoon/ Wikimedia Commons, (bottom) © LL/Roger Viollet/ Getty Images; page 16 (top) © PeterAustin/iStockphoto, (bottom) courtesy of Kzo Wikimedia Commons; page 17, © Glenda M. Powers/Shutterstock ; page 18 (top) courtesy of Steve Kirch of www.scientificamericanpast.com, (bottom) from the collection of Paul Gipe; page 19, [name of toy manufacturer]; page 20 (top) courtesy of Paul R. Jacobs of Jacobs Wind Electric Co., Inc., (bottom) courtesy of Energy Museum, Danish Museum of Energy, Bjerringbro; page 21, courtesy of NASA; page 25, © Laurence Gough/iStockphoto; page 28, © David Conniss; page 30, © Hans Laubel / iStockphoto; page 32 (top) © Hamid Gordan, www.skylight.ir, (bottom) courtesy of Quiet Revolution; page 92 (top left) 4G Technology Co., Ltd., (top right) courtesy of Quiet Revolution, (bottom) © tillsonburg/ iStockphoto; page 95, Cheryl Casey/Shutterstock.

Front cover images: top left, © Jose Ignacio Soto/iStockphoto; top middle, Dave King © Dorling Kindersley/dkimages.com; top right, © Photos.com.

INDEX